Easy Living
one-story designs ™

design basics inc.

Easy Living
one-story designs™

is a publication of:

Design Basics, Inc. • 11112 John Galt Boulevard
Omaha, NE 68137

Publisher Dennis Brozak
Associate Publisher Linda Reimer

Editor-in-Chief Bruce Arant
Associate Editors
Priscilla Ivey, Carol Stratman
Managing Editor Paul Foresman
Plans Editor Tina Leyden
Writer Carol Stratman

Art Director Sheri Potter
Graphic Designers
Yen Gutowski, Gloria A. Chavez, Kim Kegerise
Rendering Illustrators
George MacDonald, Silvia Boyd, Shawn Doherty
Research Greg Dodge
Circulation Manager Priscilla Ivey
Technical Advisor Jody Marker

President Dennis Brozak
Vice President of Operations Linda Reimer

Cover Photo: Plan #EL1748 – The Sinclair, as seen on Page 68.
Builder: Kendel Homes

Library of Congress Number: 96-092845
ISBN: 0-9647658-5-3

design basics inc.

*I*t seems there is a sense of comfort to living on one level. Maybe it's the aura of sprawling space, the absence of stairs, or the ease of passage from room to room. Whatever the case, it is clear that one-story homes not only possess an indefinable attraction, but also offer many tangible benefits to homebuyers of today: All family members sleep on the same level. Living, sleeping and eating areas can be accessed without the hassle of traveling upstairs. One-story homes have a more expansive elevation and look larger from the street than 1 ½-story or two-story homes of the same size. And without a second floor, there is freedom to enjoy taller ceiling heights in all rooms. Most importantly, one-story homes offer a unique lifestyle to their buyers - uninhibited living with the absence of steps and an abundance of horizontal space. Traditionally, one-story buyers have often been thought of as seasoned homeowners looking to retire and "move down." But that is no longer the case, as many younger buyers desire the benefits of a one-story home as well as the freedom that one-story living can provide for them. Today, as a result, one-story homes have become a preference for homebuyers of all ages.

Because of the overwhelming popularity of one-story homes, we've created Easy Living One-Story Designs™, a comprehensive selection of all 155 one-story designs from Design Basics Inc. and Carmichael & Dame. In order to help you choose the right floor plan, three very distinct collections from these two designers make up this plan book. Each collection has its own unique appeal to meet the needs and wants of individual one-story homebuyers.

HEARTLAND One-story homes from the Heartland Home Plans™ collection are value-oriented designs with the appeal of uncluttered and unpretentious living. You can find these inviting one-story homes beginning on PAGE 13.

GOLD SEAL™ One-story homes from the Gold Seal™ Home Plans collection are meant for today's buyers looking for curb appeal and a variety of amenities. This generous collection of one-story homes begins on PAGE 39.

CARMICHAEL & DAME Timeless Legacy™ one-story homes represent the best of luxury and living. To live in these homes is to truly experience the craftsmanship and intricate detailing inside them. To find these distinguished one-story homes, turn to PAGE 97.

S ince 1983, we at Design Basics have been bringing people home with many of America's most popular home plans. Our company began as a custom home plan design firm for the professional builders of our local community, Omaha, NE. As the popularity of our designs increased, we expanded our focus from designing for the local market only, to designing plans that would be adaptable anywhere. Since then, builder as well as consumer interest in our plans has grown tremendously in all 50 states and countries around the world. Today, we are one of the nation's largest home plan design services, offering a variety of home plans as well as products and services which include: color renderings, estimator's material lists, plan changes and more. (See the product review sections following each of the design collections in this book.)

Whether it's one of our home plans, a product or service, we take pride in serving you with our very best. It's all a part of our culminating efforts to lead people to their dreams of home.

Design Basics – "Bringing People Home."

The Question At Hand

Stock Home Plans vs. Your Local Architect

You've seen them before. Pages upon pages of stock home plans in books and magazines in bookstores and at the grocery store newsstand – each design posing as "the home of your dreams." But what are the benefits of using one of these stock plans in building your new home? And why should you consider choosing a stock plan over a custom-drawn design from a local architect?

For most, there are three main reasons, the first being:

Cost

There are many ways to save money when building a new home – forgoing the more expensive carpet in the bathroom or compromising with a less-costly brand of kitchen cabinets, etc. Yet, many home buyers may not know they can save a considerable amount on their home *before* it's built by using a stock plan.

How Much? On average one can expect to save $1000 or more! Typically, customdesigned plans can cost $1 - $2 per square foot. So, for a 2000' home you could expect to pay an average of $3000. In comparison, a

Design Basics home plan of the same size would cost $535.

In order to achieve the "perfect" design, it's fairly common for our customers to request customized plan changes. Such changes might include the addition of a third garage stall, the enlargement of a bedroom, alterations to the front elevation, etc. Because Design Basics plans come on erasable vellum copies, you can have changes made by your own builder or a local draftsman. Many of our customers, however, take advantage of our custom change department.

The cost of making custom changes to a Design Basics plan averages around $600. Even with the cost of custom plan changes added to the price of a plan, it's quickly evident that the dollar savings of a stock home plan can be substantial.

A second reason to consider a stock plan is:

Time

With a stock plan, you won't have to go through numerous meetings with an architect, starting from scratch to plan your home.

More information on plan #EL2652, The Lawrence, is available on page 87.

Built by: Tweedt Engineering and Construction

More information on plan #EL2461, The Shawnee, is available on page 65.

Built by: Fairview Homes

A stock plan provides a design base to start from, which consequently saves a lot of valuable time and frustration – especially if you find it difficult to visualize what you want and don't want in a home.

On top of saving time, you'll be benefitted by the fact that Design Basics puts forth a great deal of research into the development of each particular design. Every one of our plans are "thought through", to have mass appeal, while maintaining their own individual personality. And in our mobile society, this factor alone makes the resale value of homes built from our plans that much better.

Third and finally, you'll be benefitted by a stock plan if you're looking for the latest in:

Design Trends

What's "in", it seems, changes as quickly as the new home products that emerge each year. And unless you've made it a hobby, you may have a hard time keeping up with the newest, "exciting" ways to use space in a home. In this, stock design services have a unique advantage. At Design Basics, we continually hear from home builders as well as homebuyers regarding what's "in" and

what's "out". Plus, we can suggest ideas regarding custom plan changes that are currently most popular for any of our designs.

Having mentioned some of the benefits of buying a stock home plan, we at Design Basics invite you to call us with any additional questions you might have. We're here to help you discover the design that's right for *your* specific needs and desires. It's just a part of our company's mission – *"Bringing People Home."*

You're looking for plans for your next new home.

You're looking for plans for your next new home. You don't want to build from just *any* home plan. You want a design that truly meets your needs – one that looks the way you *want* it to look, with a livable, functional floor plan. In a world of home plans filled with countless configurations of room arrangements, elevation styles and square footage options, how do you find a design that's really *right* for you?

More information on plan #EL2290, The Monterey, is available on page 59.

Finding the home plan thats right for you

Built by: E & G Construction Unlimited

There are a number of ways you can find your dream home. Of course, studying the home plan designs in a book like this can provide a good deal of direction, and for many, the perfect solution. As you look through the following pages, you may find it helpful to write down your specific likes and dislikes regarding plans that catch your eye. Doing so can help you more clearly define your design preferences, and will better prepare you for meetings with your builder. Another very practical way to discover the kind of design you want, however, is by touring model homes, speculative homes under construction or your local parade of homes (or similar events). By doing so, you can experience the real-life livability of those homes' designs, and at the same time, discover what your local builders have to offer in the way of quality and workmanship. Plus, you are likely to be treated to the latest in products and technology.

BALANCE THE RATIONAL AND EMOTIONAL APPEAL OF A DESIGN.

If you have the opportunity to actually tour new homes for design ideas, do your best to keep a balanced perspective. It may be difficult, but it's essential to look beyond the decorating and determine first whether or not the home's floor plan works for your individual needs. Especially with regard to parade and model homes, everything inside and out is carefully thought through in order to evoke "oohs" and "aahs" from attendees. Rather than being swept away by the beauty of the marble, the impressive media wall, or other "emotional pulls", focus on how the rooms flow together. Weigh your impressions of the home's overall design in the context of your own daily lifestyle.

"Our home has to be a one-level design with a master suite thats well-separated..."

"Plus three baths..."

"... a formal dining room..."

DEFINE THE IDEAL HOME

As you compile your likes and dislikes of specific design elements in this book, and/or from visiting model homes, prepare your own definition of the *ideal* home – one that would best meet your immediate, as well as future needs. Begin by making a wish list that includes such specifics as: "Our home has to be a one-level design with a master suite that's well-separated from three other bedrooms. Plus, three baths, a formal dining room and a separate breakfast area." Or, "I'd like a space for a dining room hutch rather than one that's built-in, so I can buy that dining room set I saw last week."

Regarding your future needs, do you foresee your family growing, or perhaps caring for an aging parent? How about future job demands – do the designs you're seeing provide a space suitable for a home office? Conversely, you may not intend to live in the house for a long time. In that case, you may want to consider the resale potential of various home designs.

GET MORE FOR YOUR DOLLAR

While the cost of building a new home can often appear steep, *good design* does not have to cost a lot. Of course, any home's design should first be livable, but to optimize your investment, every inch of square footage should be utilized to the best of its potential. This is achieved with good traffic patterns for everyday living. For example, quick access from the garage to the kitchen helps when bringing in groceries, while easy access from the kitchen to the dining room is a must for carrying hot dishes. The proximity of the family room (or great room in some designs) to the kitchen should also be considered since many people spend the majority of their time in these two areas.

Anyone wanting to get more for their money in a home should also look for designs with built-in features. These features, such as a hutch, desk, pantry, bookshelves and entertainment centers, spare you from losing square footage to furniture, and therefore have become popular amenities.

You may also want to consider a home plan with expansion or bonus room possibilities. Often, especially in homes with a second level, a design lends itself to the availability of adding a bonus room above the garage. In one-story designs, finished basements are often a viable option for an additional bedroom or playroom for the kids. To keep costs down initially, such spaces may be left unfinished and used for storage.

So how do you find the home plan that's absolutely right for you? Ultimately, only *you* are qualified to define the "perfect" design. Industry experts can offer suggestions and opinions, and builders can showcase their finest efforts in parades and model homes, but it is you who must weigh all the options and decide,

"While easy access from the kitchen... "

"The proximity of the family room..."

"... bonus room possibilities... "

When a home plan would be perfect if only you could ...

Change It

Finding a home plan that's right for you can be as easy as flipping through the pages of a plan book like this one. With so many designs to choose from, it's hard *not* to come across a plan you find appealing. In fact, it's likely you'll discover a *number* of plans you really like, but if you're typical of many who comb through plan books, you may still hear yourself saying, "It's the perfect floor plan, but ..."

> "... if only the kitchen were larger."
>
> "... it only has three bedrooms and we need four."
>
> "... I need a three-car garage and this one has only two stalls."
>
> "... I don't like the use of stone on the front elevation."

Such reasons shouldn't be ones to turn you away from an otherwise good home plan design. Making modifications to a home plan you've selected may be just the solution to finding the "perfect" home design. At Design Basics, we are committed to making sure our home plans fit your needs. That's why we have an entire Custom Change Division devoted to making modifications to and answering technical questions about our home plans. Our Custom Change Division frees you from the potential hassles of trying to arrange modifications to your Design Basics home plan on your own. As a "one-stop shop", you can purchase your home plan and have us make the alterations you desire. It's one way we can assure your Design Basics home plan will be the "perfect" plan– right from the start. Some of the most common custom changes to our home plans include:

Common Custom Changes

- Modifying or designing alternate front elevations
- Changing basement foundations to slab or crawlspace
- Converting exterior 2x4 walls to 2x6 walls
- Modifying 8-foot main level walls to 9-foot main level walls
- Stretching individual room sizes
- Changing garage specifications – from front-load to side-load; and from 2-car to 3-car (or more)
- Modifying foundations to include walk-out basements

Above: The Sinclair as originally designed
Built by: Kendel Homes

Facing Page: The Sinclair with the garage changed to a side-load.
Built by: Wegher, Petersen, Schultzen Home Builders

More information on plan #EL1748, The Sinclair, is available on page 68.

While these changes are among the most common, many other modifications, including adding rooms or finished basements, are also viable options for changing a home plan. Just about any type of plan modification is possible. As you consider modifying a plan, however, be mindful of the fact that moving walls will change the basic structure of the home and that the layout of other areas in the home may be affected. For this reason, our Customer Support and Custom Change Specialists are always happy to discuss your ideas over the phone. Call toll free 7:00 a.m. – 6:00 p.m. CT at the number listed below. In most cases, custom plan change consultation and price quotes are provided absolutely free of charge.

Visualize it

When you discover a design that *does* meet all your needs, it still may be difficult for you to visualize what the home will look like from all sides, and whether or not the individual room sizes are adequate. To help you visualize our home plans, we offer the Study Print & Furniture Layout Guide™. This helpful, easy-to-use resource was specially designed for plan buyers like yourself, to help make sure that the plan you select is exactly right for your needs. Included is a Study Print, which shows all four of the home's exterior views, as well as the roof layout. Plus, we include the Furniture Layout Guide which features a 1/4"–scale rendered floor plan specific to your selected Design Basics design, along with over 100 adhesive-backed, reusable 1/4"–scale furniture pieces. Proportionate to typical furniture sizes, the pieces will help you visualize furniture in your new home and help determine whether you'll desire plan modifications.

So, when looking at home plans throughout the following pages, don't overlook those that aren't quite "perfect." Consider a custom plan change or our fun-to-use Study Print & Furniture Layout Guide™. You'll hear yourself saying, "This IS the perfect floor plan!"

· ·

For a free quote on a Design Basics custom change or to purchase a plan-specific Study Print & Furniture Layout Guide™ for only $29.95, contact on of our Customer Support Specialists.

Call us direct
1-800-947-7526

Helpful Tools you shouldn't build your new home without.

For many home buyers, visualizing the finished home is a challenge. Our **Study Print & Furniture Layout Guide** makes it easy. First, the Study Print provides views of all exterior elevations. Secondly, the Furniture Layout Guide provides you a "feel" for room sizes, with a 1/4"–scale floor plan, over 100 reusable furniture pieces and helpful tips on space planning. Available for any Design Basics plan. Please see order form.

Only $29.95

Can I afford to buy it ?

For many of us as home buyers, the price of building a new home enters our minds in two contexts:

1) Can I afford to buy it?
   and/or
2) Do I want to pay that price for this house?

Unless we are licensed appraisers, most of us rarely think about what makes up the cost of the new home. And if we really knew, we might be surprised to find out where the money we are spending is actually going.

The information below breaks down the cost of a detached, single-family home based on national averages from a recent *Builders Survey of Construction Costs* – a survey of 50 nationwide builders in 37 metro areas, conducted by the National Association of Home Builders, and averages from the *Marshall Valuation Service* – a manual used by licensed appraisers.

Construction Costs	
(Materials & Labor)	55 - 60%
Finished Lot Costs	25 - 30%
Financing Costs	2 - 5%
Overhead & General Expenses	5 - 7%
Marketing Costs	2 - 5%
Sales Commission	3 - 6%
Profit	8 - 10%

The named figures are *national averages* only, and may not accurately represent your local market. In fact, there may be many things that could affect the price of your new home. Two of the more prominent factors are regulatory costs and level of amenities.

REGULATION

The issue of regulatory fees, environmental or otherwise, has been a heated topic of debate for all involved in the home building industry for some time. The reason is that environmental and/or state and local regulations in some cases *significantly* impact the cost of new construction in certain areas of the country. In the *Builders Survey of Construction Costs* used in the evaluation at left, Wetland Preservation and Impact Fees were included in the cost of the Finished Lot. The *Builders Survey* concluded that 6.5% of the total cost of the lot, or roughly 1.8% of the total cost of the home, could be attributed to the price of these fees. However, in certain areas of the country, builders have claimed to attribute anywhere from 8 - 16% of the total cost of a home to regulatory costs. That means that for a $120,000 home, as much as $19,200 could be attributed to regulatory costs!

Regulations vary on the state and local levels, but federal regulations effect everyone. Some of the most common federal regulations that impact new construction include: the Clean Water Act, the Endangered Species Act and Occupational Safety and Health Administration regulations. Many local and state regulations also impact the construction of new homes, such as growth controls, restrictive zoning and impact fees.

Why do new home

Depending on where you live, regulation may have a very significant or insignificant affect on the price of your home. If you are interested in knowing the affect of regulatory fees in your area, contact your local builder or local municipal offices for more information.

AMENITIES

The materials that go into the price of a new home comprise a large percentage of its cost. Since both builders and buyers affect the kind and quality of materials that go into a home (lumber, floor coverings, paint, etc.), it is important to be especially aware of how these elements can affect its price.

When figuring out how much a new home will cost, the common practice has been to price the home out on a "cost per square foot" basis. As a result, buyers often take a home plan, either one from a plan book or one they'd already purchased, to various builders for bids.

In recent years, with the variety, type and quality of amenities rapidly increasing, many builders have found the "cost per square foot" analysis to be inadequate in successfully giving buyers what they are really looking for. The problem with pricing a home on such a basis is that the different bids given by builders may not be "apples for apples" comparisons. For example, one builder may offer better quality or higher allowances for appliances, lighting fixtures, etc. in their bid than another. Also, many features that builders consider their "standard" amenities often vary greatly. One builder may make it his practice to provide energy-efficient heating and cooling systems in all of his homes, which will cost more money.

Another builder may make it his practice to "exceed" local code requirements in all areas of the home.

In the same vain, the specific brand and quality of features you choose to put in your home will also dramatically affect the price. It is estimated that lighting fixtures will cost the average home buyer around three percent of the total cost of their home. But if a buyer decides that he or she "must have" a $5,000 chandelier in their entryway, the cost of their lighting fixtures and the total cost of their home will be significantly impacted. The same goes for any appliances, doors, cabinetry, flooring materials etc. that are chosen for a home. That's why two homes with the same square footage can have such dramatic cost differences.

So what's the best thing to do as a home buyer to ensure a fair price on a new home? Make sure the bids you receive are apples for apples comparisons. Find out as much as you can about each builder's product. Tour other homes they've built. Find out as much *specific* information as you can about standard allowances, finishes, grades of carpet and lighting fixtures, paint, brick, plumbing and heating systems. Consider how long a builder has been in business and the quality of his homes. Compare one builder's standard products to another's.

Being aware of where your money is going can be a comforting factor as a new home buyer. And taking into consideration the level of amenities and regulations that might affect its price will help you prepare for a successful building process.

ost what they do **?**

PANEL COMPONENT CONSTRUCTION

Before

Panelized construction or panel component construction– a method of building a home with a series of pre-assembled sections– has been around longer than many of us might think. In the 1800's, Mark Twain (Samuel Clemens) had his own home shipped down the Mississippi in the form of panels. Today, the popularity of panelized construction is taking hold nationwide as a viable, competitively-priced alternative for builders and home buyers alike.

Years ago, various forms of manufactured housing became quite popular in this country, namely through the development of mobile homes and pre-fabricated houses. Unfortunately, many of these homes were low-quality structures, and as a result, much of the buying public formed negative perceptions of manufactured housing in general. In recent years, however, new technologies and better construction techniques have improved the quality of panelized homes in a number of ways.

Today, it is not only possible to attain the home of your dreams through panelized construction, but you can also save both time and money.

The process of building a home via panelized construction is beneficial to builders and home buyers in a number of ways. First, it solves several problems facing the home building industry which are the result of a serious shortage of skilled subcontractors. Difficulties for a builder in securing qualified subcontractors can result in costly delays on the job site. Since panelized homes go up relatively quickly – panel by panel, rather than board by board – it saves builders and home buyers time in the construction process. And because the lumber in a panelized home is exposed to the weather for a much shorter period of time, it is not as likely to suffer damage due to the elements.

Besides lower quality, another misconception associated with panelized construction is that buyers may be forced to accept dated, generic designs. Many of today's panelized companies can execute even the most elegant home plan designs with sophisticated roof systems, such as those from Design Basics. And, these homes are just as energy-efficient as homes that are typically "stick built." In fact, in some cases they may be more so.

The National Association of Home Builders (NAHB) Research Center estimates that in building an average 2,000 square foot home using conventional construction techniques, approximately 4,000 pounds of wood and drywall end up in the dumpster. Such construction waste is expensive. Adding to the materials cost, construction waste disposal adds hundreds of dollars to the price of a new home. Along with minimizing waste, computer-engineered panels and factory-controlled building conditions help ensure square, plumb walls and accurate floor and roof systems. And oftentimes builders, as a result, are better able to provide a more accurate projected price to the home buyer.

After ...

Upon delivery to the job site, the extent to which the building components (wall panels, roof trusses, floor joists, etc.), are completed, varies from company to company in the panelized industry. Some companies fully frame, insulate, sheath, and place windows in the exterior wall panels of the home. Other companies merely provide framed walls, allowing the insulation, sheathing, drywall, etc. to be added on later.

If you would like more information about panelized home manufacturers or experienced panelized builders who build Design Basics plans in your area, contact one of our Customer Support Specialists at (800)947-7526.

Built by: Maple Woods Construction

More information on plan #EL2173, The Fraser, is available on page 47.

Heartland Home Plans™

One-story homes from the Heartland Home Plans™ collection are a part of a philosophy based on designing homes for true practicality and livability. The elevations of these homes are unpretentious, warm and immediately welcoming. They are characterized by uncomplicated rooflines, clean, sharp gables and traditional elements such as brick and lap siding, and front porches to help create a softer, more inviting look from the street. The design of each floor plan allows for flexibility in the selection of materials and amenities. The floor plans as a whole center on buyers' everyday lifestyles, so one can easily imagine themselves cooking in the kitchen, watching television in the family room and getting ready for the day in the master suite. Regardless of a home's square footage, each floor plan is efficient in its use of space. Together, all of these factors make Heartland one-story homes a true value for those who will live in them. The following pages introduce 44 designs from this collection. They are practical as well as easily adaptable to individual lifestyles. It makes sense to live in them - which is what one wants most out of a great design.

THE DASHING MORTON GROVE

In the great room, a cathedral ceiling for a feeling of openness, and a fireplace for a sense of welcome. The snack bar in the kitchen, to serve or eat upon. Two bathrooms, one exclusive to the master suite and the other easily serving the secondary bedroom and all other areas of the home.

• ORDER NO. EL 8161 - PRICE CODE 11

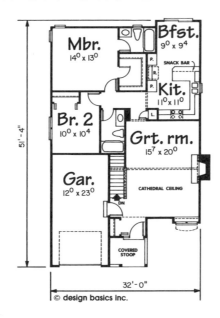

Mbr.
14⁰ x 13⁰

Bfst.
9⁰ x 9⁴

SNACK BAR

Kit.
11⁰ x 11⁰

Br. 2
10⁰ x 10⁴

Grt. rm.
15⁷ x 20⁰

Gar.
12⁰ x 23⁰

CATHEDRAL CEILING

DN

COVERED STOOP

51' - 4"

32' - 0"

© design basics inc.

Total Square Footage: 1162 Dimensions: Width 32 - 0" Depth 51' - 4"

THE SHAPE OF TRINITY ACRES

The fireplace in the great room, equally at home on formal and informal occasions. Two pantries helping to organize the kitchen. And the master suite placed at the back of the home for an easy get-away spot.

• ORDER NO. EL 8163 - PRICE CODE 11

Total Square Footage: 1162 Dimensions: Width 39' - 4" Depth 53' - 4"

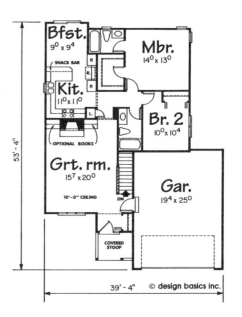

Bfst.
9⁰ x 9⁴

SNACK BAR

Mbr.
14⁰ x 13⁰

Kit.
11⁰ x 11⁰

OPTIONAL BOOKS

Br. 2
10⁰ x 10⁴

Grt. rm.
15⁷ x 20⁰

10'-0" CEILING

DN

Gar.
19⁴ x 25⁰

COVERED STOOP

53' - 4"

39' - 4"

© design basics inc.

THE UNCOMPLICATED KIRBY FARM

Living, eating and cooking areas designated as the center of activity in open, unrestricted space. Other features: a front coat closet for guests; a closet for hanging clothes in the laundry room; and a large master suite closet with room for storage and a sizeable wardrobe.

• ORDER NO. EL 8093 - PRICE CODE 12

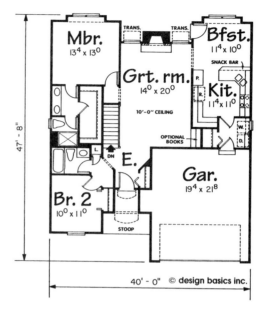

Total Square Footage: 1212 Dimensions: Width 40' - 0" Depth 47' - 8"

THE RELAXED STYLE OF REDWOOD LANE

One bedroom for an empty-nest lifestyle. A front porch fostering the desire to retire to it at the end of the day. A touch of formality in the dining room. And a kitchen, breakfast area and great room connected for the pleasure of living there.

• ORDER NO. EL 8128 - PRICE CODE 12

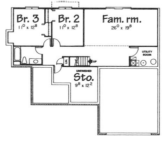

Total Square Footage: 1279 Dimensions: Width 52' - 8" Depth 46' - 0" Optional Finished Basement 984 Sq. Ft.

THE SUBTLETY OF SUMMIT POINT

An angled snack bar in the kitchen to offer an alternative to sitting at the table. Windows in the great room providing a view to the back, and enhancing the ambience of the fireplace. A separate bedroom wing for seclusion and privacy in three bedrooms.

• ORDER NO. EL 8092 - PRICE CODE 12

Total Square Footage: 1295 Dimensions: Width 52' - 0" Depth 44' - 0"

THE SPUNK OF SABINO CANYON

On the elevation, a porch for greeting those walking by. An angled entry, to provide intrigue to those walking in. Counters wrapping around the kitchen, making themselves useful in a variety of ways. And a spacious family room at the rear, providing an area to enjoy a fire and a terrific view.

• ORDER NO. EL 8164 - PRICE CODE 13

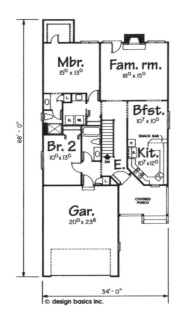

Total Square Footage: 1333 Dimensions: Width 34' - 0" Depth 68' - 0"

A Vision Of Winter Woods

A wide covered stoop noticeably substantial enough for a chair. Wrapping counters in the kitchen to help quickly access all that is needed to cook. The benefit of a large walk-in closet, sunlit tub and dual-sink vanity, giving the master suite its own private space.

• Order No. EL 8091 - Price Code 13

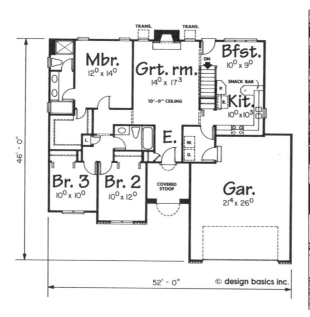

Total Square Footage: 1360 Dimensions: Width 52' - 0" Depth 46' - 0"

Life In The Gabriel Bay

Office space or hobby room options in two secondary bedrooms. Room for meals and entertaining in the kitchen/breakfast area coupled with the great room. In the master retreat, a corner tub for basking in relaxation.

• Order No. EL 8013 - Price Code 13

1-800-947-7526
Order Direct

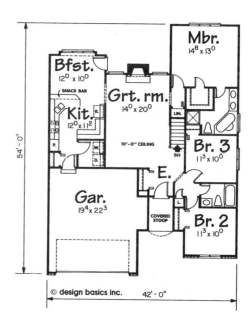

Total Square Footage: 1392 Dimensions: Width 42' - 0" Depth 54' - 0"

THE SLEEK SARASOTA FALLS

An expandable dinette for larger groups. The privately located family room with tall windows, for a clear view of nature. A back porch to watch the children play in the yard. And a snack bar to accommodate a buffet meal.

• ORDER No. EL 8165 - PRICE CODE 13

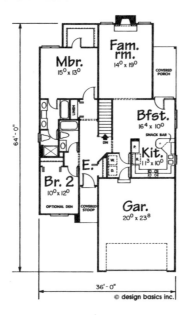

Total Square Footage: 1398 Dimensions: Width 36 - 0" Depth 64' - 0"

A HOME FOR TODAY - THE CEDAR FALLS

An expansive great room with sloped ceiling, adding character to conversations there. Two eating areas - the dining room open to the great room for entertaining and the breakfast area open to the casual air of the kitchen.

• ORDER No. EL 8129 - PRICE CODE 14

1-800-947-7526
Order Direct

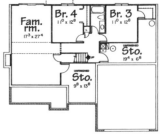

Total Square Footage: 1420 Dimensions: Width 52' - 8" Depth 46' - 0" Optional Finished Basement 994 Sq. Ft.

THE ALLURE OF CHANDLER HILLS

Arches and columns on a front porch dedicated to summer. A tall, sloping great room ceiling to naturally prompt warm comments from guests who relax there. And the master suite at the rear of the home for secluded peace and quiet.

• ORDER No. EL 8089 - PRICE CODE 14

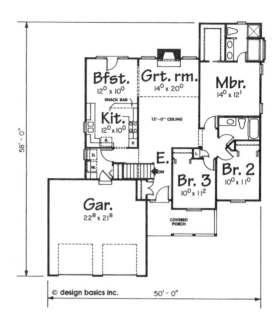

Total Square Footage: 1433 Dimensions: Width 50' - 0" Depth 58' - 0"

THE PLENTIFUL BRADFORD POINTE

Two porches for sipping summertime drinks with leisure. A secluded bedroom wing for quiet places to retire to. And easy connection between the living areas, making daily traffic uninhibited.

• ORDER No. EL 8160 - PRICE CODE 14

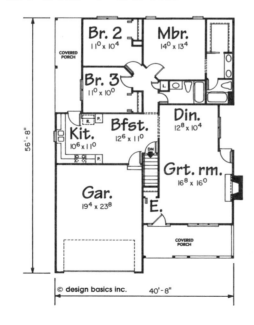

Total Square Footage: 1449 Dimensions: Width 40' - 8" Depth 56' - 8"

A Longing For Spring Valley

A front covered porch to escape and dream upon. In the kitchen, an island counter for added space to prepare and cook meals. A large dinette open to both formal and informal eating. And a master bedroom with the option of a second closet if needed.

• Order No. EL 8090 - Price Code 14

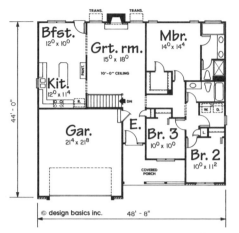

Total Square Footage: 1453 Dimensions: Width 48 - 8" Depth 44' - 0" Optional Master Bedroom

Experience The Copper Creek

A large dining and great room located together - perfect for parties. An organized kitchen that easily accesses the garage and dinette. A rear covered deck to commune with nature. And two secondary bedrooms for overnight family and guests.

• Order No. EL 8015 - Price Code 15

Total Square Footage: 1515 Dimensions: Width 52' - 0" Depth 48' - 8"

A View Of The Shadow Pines

Sloped ceiling in the great room and warmth by a crackling fireplace. Patio doors in the breakfast area for leading to backyard fun and letting in sunshine. And bayed dining room windows adding definition to memories created there.

• Order No. EL 8088 - Price Code 15

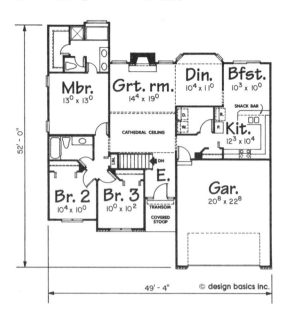

Total Square Footage: 1520 Dimensions: Width 49' - 4" Depth 52' - 0"

The Attractive Skyline Woods

A large great room for when the family comes home. Two secondary bedrooms for sleeping areas or places to explore a hobby. Streamlined traffic from garage to kitchen for unloading the car after grocery shopping.

• Order No. EL 8159 - Price Code 15

1-800-947-7526
Order Direct

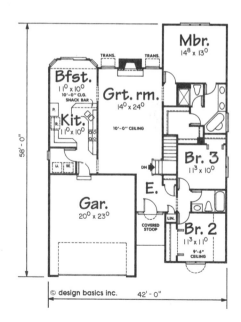

Total Square Footage: 1562 Dimensions: Width 42' - 0" Depth 58' - 0"

THE CLEAN SPIRIT OF COLLINS FALLS

A dining room that becomes expandable space for the great room and vice-versa. A third bedroom flexible as a den for those who need an office or a quiet place to wind down. A bayed breakfast area to offer plenty of sunlight for cooking and eating.

• ORDER No. EL 8087 - PRICE CODE 15

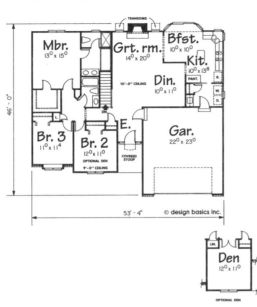

Total Square Footage: 1579 Dimensions: Width 53' - 4" Depth 46' - 0" Optional Den

THE ADJUSTABLE JACOBS BAY

An optional walk-out basement for extra bedrooms, storage and living space. A spacious island kitchen for the one who loves to cook. And an entertaining area that's versatile for holidays and gatherings.

• ORDER No. EL 8158 - PRICE CODE 15

1-800-947-7526
Order Direct

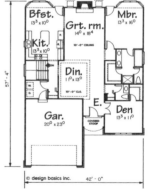

Total Square Footage: 1593 Dimensions: Width 42' - 0" Depth 57' - 4" Optional Finished Basement 1137 Sq. Ft.

THE SENSIBILITY OF MAPLE GROVE

An island counter in the kitchen to help prepare meals for cooking and serving. Formal and informal eating areas near each other convenient as extra space when larger groups stay to eat. Three bedrooms for families to dream away the night.

• ORDER NO. EL 8080 - PRICE CODE 16

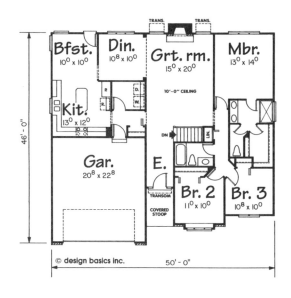

Total Square Footage: 1628 Dimensions: Width 50' - 0" Depth 46' - 0"

A FLAIR OF ITS OWN - THE BELLE HARBOR

For a sense of unity, the entry, dining room and great room with 11-foot ceilings. In the master bath, his and her vanities and a corner soaking tub for a feeling of luxury. And a lazy welcome to the outdoors on a long back porch.

• ORDER NO. EL 8079 - PRICE CODE 16

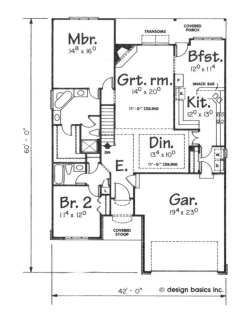

Total Square Footage: 1633 Dimensions: Width 42' - 0" Depth 60' - 0"

A Way Of Life - The Jennys Brook

Separated sleeping quarters, for the young and old alike to get away from it all. Views of the outdoors or a glowing fireplace in the great room. The kitchen, wide and complete with a peninsula snack bar for meals on the go.

• Order No. EL 8016- Price Code 16

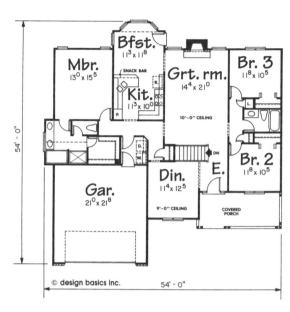

Total Square Footage: 1691 Dimensions: Width 54' - 0" Depth 54' - 0"

The Varied Sonora Springs

A den with French doors doubling as a bedroom. A walk-through kitchen to freely access more areas of the main floor. A back porch, adding leisure space to the master bedroom. And an expandable great room and dining room so there's room for everyone.

• Order No. EL 8168 - Price Code 17

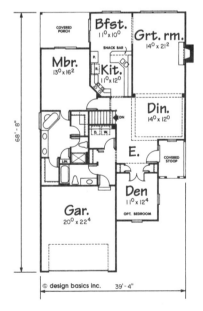

Total Square Footage: 1705 Dimensions: Width 39' - 4" Depth 68' - 8" Optional Bedroom

A SENSE OF THE NORTH CLIFFS

Back and front covered porches – one for talking with the neighbors and the other for barbeques. A snack bar island counter and extra counter space along one wall, all helping the kitchen more efficiently serve the eating areas. A comfortable place to kick back beneath a cathedral ceiling in the great room.

• ORDER NO. EL 8078 - PRICE CODE 17

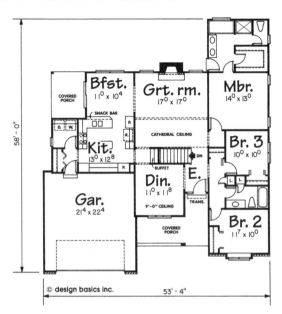

Total Square Footage: 1707 Dimensions: Width 53' - 4" Depth 58' - 0"

THE RELAXATION OF QUAIL HOLLOW

A great room that welcomes hearty discussion. A snack bar in the kitchen - the perfect place, it seems, for one to sit and chat while another bakes. And a back porch to view an Autumn sunset.

• ORDER NO. EL 8069 - PRICE CODE 17

1-800-947-7526
Order Direct

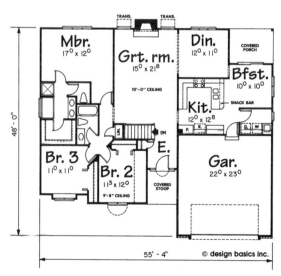

Total Square Footage: 1729 Dimensions: Width 55' - 4" Depth 48' - 0"

THE OPENNESS OF HANCOCK RIDGE

A friendly covered porch to watch the play in the front yard. A half wall in the dining room for views into the great room while eating. And a spacious laundry room to accommodate three bedrooms - separated into two wings for privacy within the home itself.

• Order No. EL 8068 - Price Code 17

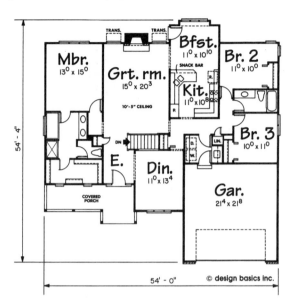

Total Square Footage: 1751 Dimensions: Width 54' - 0" Depth 54' - 4"

THE CASUAL ATMOSPHERE OF RIVER OAKS

A deep front porch leaving room for a swing and quiet evening meditation. A dining room that can expand into the great room for large gatherings. And two secondary bedrooms with distinct windows providing views to the front.

• Order No. EL 8067 - Price Code 17

1-800-947-7526
Order Direct

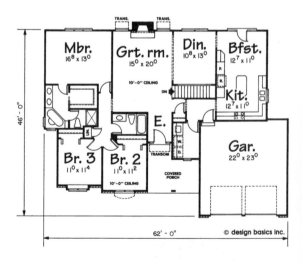

Total Square Footage: 1775 Dimensions: Width 62' - 0" Depth 46' - 0"

THE EXUBERANCE OF HIDDEN ACRES

A generous kitchen with a snack bar for an informal meal. Bayed windows to harness and beautify incoming light in the breakfast area. A large master suite with a dressing area conveniently offering a dual-sink vanity. And a Hollywood bath for two spacious secondary bedrooms.

• ORDER NO. EL 8066 - PRICE CODE 18

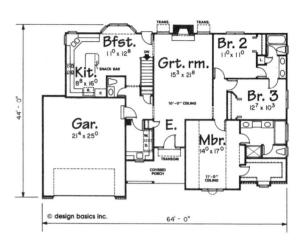

Total Square Footage: 1805 Dimensions: Width 64' - 0" Depth 44' - 0"

THE COMFORTABLE PLEASURE OF FOREST GLEN

A cathedral ceiling in the great room to enhance just about everything done there. A covered porch off the breakfast area, suggesting a little sun and air after meals. And a wealth of essentials in the master suite – a large closet, open shelves, a dual-sink vanity and sunlit tub.

• ORDER NO. EL 8018 - PRICE CODE 18

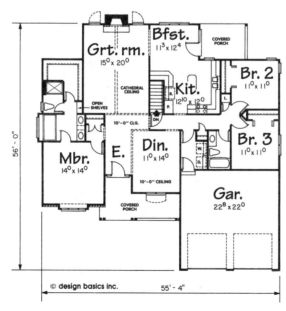

Total Square Footage: 1815 Dimensions: Width 55' - 4" Depth 56' - 0"

THE COMFORTABLY REFINED INDIAN SPRINGS

Shutters, double-hung windows and a distinct covered porch to coax outsiders in. Ten-foot ceilings in all living areas of the home to free any feelings of restriction. And a master bath with abundant vanity and dressing space.

• ORDER NO. EL 8059 - PRICE CODE 18

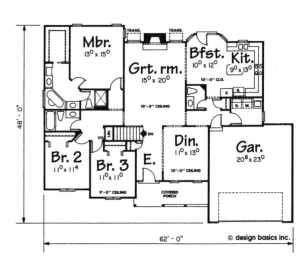

Total Square Footage: 1842 Dimensions: Width 62 - 0" Depth 48' - 0"

A FEEL FOR MORGAN CREEK

A generous serving buffet, adjacent to the dining room for serving formal meals; and a snack bar in the kitchen for serving informal meals. An extensive great room serving a variety of functions – a path to the bedroom wing, a possible extension of the dining room and a cozy place for an after-dinner cup of coffee.

• ORDER NO. EL 8058 - PRICE CODE 18

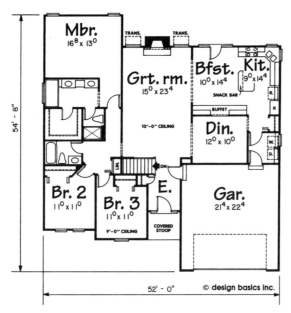

Total Square Footage: 1852 Dimensions: Width 52' - 0" Depth 54' - 8"

The Peace And Freedom Of Hunters Crossing

An angled see-through fireplace, perfect for many to enjoy in the great room or just a few in the more intimate hearth room. Wrapping counters and a snack bar in the kitchen for easy cooking and serving. Separate wings for the bedrooms, leaving options open for office space or serious hobbies.

• Order No. EL 8019 - Price Code 19

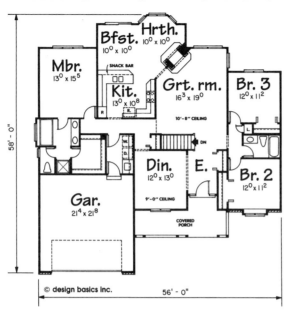

Total Square Footage: 1919 Dimensions: Width 56' - 0" Depth 58' - 0"

The Fundamentals Of Laurel Grove

An elegant dining room that offers the entry a pleasant view. An island kitchen, that from the sink area, sees the family room. And a desk in the breakfast area for a sunny place to balance the checkbook.

• Order No. EL 8046 - Price Code 19

1-800-947-7526
Order Direct

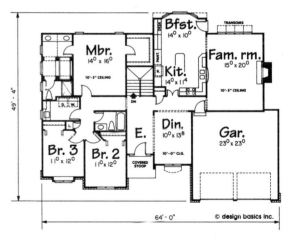

Total Square Footage: 1967 Dimensions: Width 64' - 0" Depth 49' - 4"

Design Basics Inc. — 29 —

THE FAMILIARITY OF MILLERS WAY

A covered porch prone to lure one outside during a soft summer rain. Tall windows and ceiling in the dining room, adding to the thoughts of ham and turkey dinners there. Along the wall joining the kitchen and breakfast area, counter space and a desk - places for household planning or homework.

• ORDER NO. EL 8047 - PRICE CODE 19

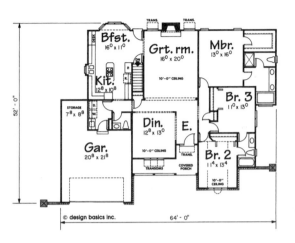

Total Square Footage: 1999 Dimensions: Width 64' - 0" Depth 52' - 0"

THE AIRINESS OF ALBERTA FALLS

A covered front porch, expanding the welcome of the elevation. An entry open to the dining room and stairway for a view of elegance once inside. At the back of the home, a spacious family room, breakfast area and kitchen.

• ORDER NO. EL 8122 - PRICE CODE 20

1-800-947-7526
Order Direct

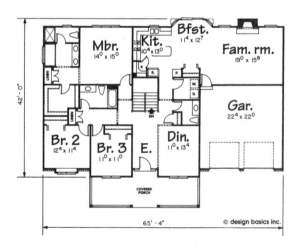

Total Square Footage: 2042 Dimensions: Width 65' - 4" Depth 42' - 0"

THE IMPACT OF CROOKED CREEK

Large formal rooms for the space to entertain. A fireplace and picture window to enhance family activity in the great room. A well-placed counter in the kitchen to help easier serve meals in the dining room. And in the master suite, a sitting area with abundant sunlight for relaxing or working.

• ORDER NO. EL 8118 - PRICE CODE 20

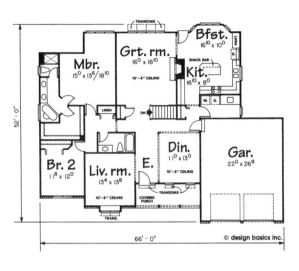

Total Square Footage: 2079 Dimensions: Width 66'- 0" Depth 52'- 0"

THE ATTRACTION OF THE PRAIRIE VIEW

A 10-foot dining room ceiling to add elegance to a formal meal. For admiring nature, windows all along the great room, hearth room and breakfast area. And a three-sided fireplace to project warmth to these areas - whether eating or just relaxing.

• ORDER NO. EL 8022- PRICE CODE 21

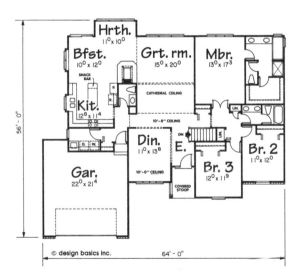

Total Square Footage: 2117 Dimensions: Width 64' - 0" Depth 56' - 0"

THE FLOW OF HARVEST RUN

Two living spaces – a family room secluded for day-to-day living, and a living room open for easy entertaining. The kitchen, with wrapping counters, is perfectly situated to serve the dining room and breakfast area. Separate bedroom wings offer privacy and options to convert bedrooms into living space.

• ORDER NO. EL 8119 - PRICE CODE 21

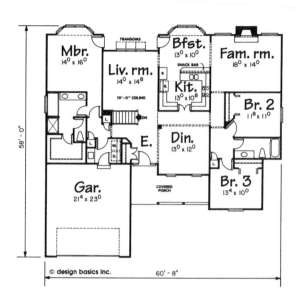

Total Square Footage: 2144 Dimensions: Width 60' - 8" Depth 58' - 0"

THE GENEROUS COOPERS FARM

A breezy front porch to sit upon and catch up with the day. Office space with a separate outdoor entrance for clients. The kitchen, breakfast area and great room, freely open to one another. And a lovely window in the master suite, providing a view of the back as well as a good light source for reading.

• ORDER NO. EL 8045 - PRICE CODE 21

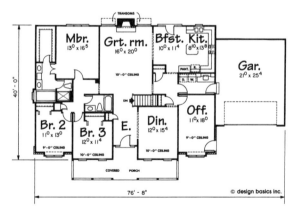

Total Square Footage: 2151 Dimensions: Width 76'- 8" Depth 40'- 0"

THE QUAINT PIZAZZ OF NELSONS LANDING

French doors to seclude the den in peace and quiet. A bayed breakfast area with access to the back for some fresh air after a meal. And in the master bedroom, a compartmented dressing area that doesn't compromise the need for space.

• ORDER NO. EL 8121 - PRICE CODE 22

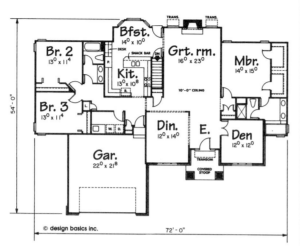

Total Square Footage: 2241 Dimensions: Width 72' - 0" Depth 54' - 0"

THE NOTABLE JACKSON ACRES

A wide, columned, unforgettable stoop. A tall entry and even taller great room for day-to-day living. Meal preparation in the kitchen and eating in the breakfast area amidst the cozy ambience of a see-through fireplace.

• ORDER NO. EL 8017 - PRICE CODE 22

1-800-947-7526 Order Direct

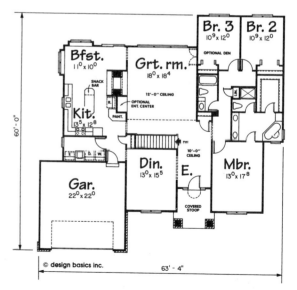

Total Square Footage: 2246 Dimensions: Width 63' - 4" Depth 60' - 0"

THE DAZZLING EFFECT OF EMERALD HARBOR

At the back, open and free living space. A breakfast area for eating or leading to backyard play. A corner fireplace, prone to draw people into the family room to sit by it and ponder the flames. And a master suite designed for thoughts of romance and privacy.

• ORDER NO. EL 8120 - PRICE CODE 22

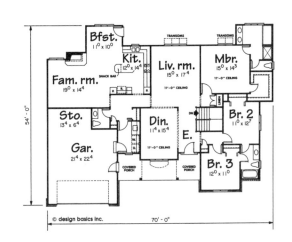

Total Square Footage: 2293 Dimensions: Width 70' - 0" Depth 54' - 0"

THE FINELY FINISHED SYDNEY LANE

A great room and hearth room to choose between for a sit by the fire. Two porches, each providing their own aspects of the outdoors. And a master suite adorned with two sets of French doors placing a sense of romance in the air.

• ORDER NO. EL 8048 - PRICE CODE 22

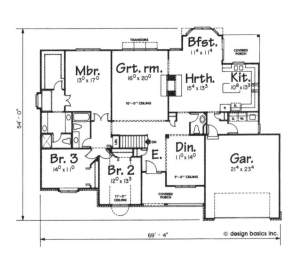

Total Square Footage: 2298 Dimensions: Width 69' - 4" Depth 54' - 0"

THE PATTERNS OF FALCON POINT

A front porch to while away an afternoon on - or to dream of doing so. Three big bedrooms with room for more than just sleep. A see-through fireplace that has gathered the living areas of the home around it, helping to bring those who live there together too.

• ORDER NO. EL 8044 - PRICE CODE 24

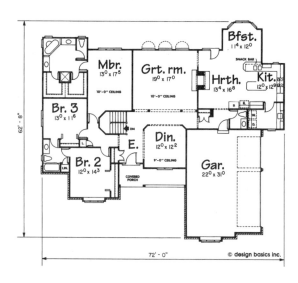

Total Square Footage: 2404 Dimensions: Width 72' - 0" Depth 62' - 8"

ENRICHED WITH LIVING - EAGLES RIDGE

Stone and shake exterior for the feeling of a snug cottage. Formal rooms linked for entertaining ease. Kitchen, breakfast area and family room arranged for seclusion - leaving ample freedom for family leisure. Also, a private wing of four bedroom retreats.

• ORDER NO. EL 8023 - PRICE CODE 24

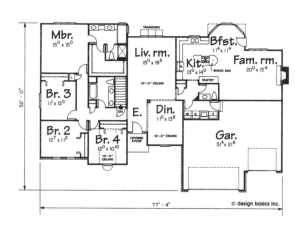

Total Square Footage: 2467 Dimensions: Width 77' - 4" Depth 52' - 0"

Heartland Home Plans™  Product Review

EXERCISE YOUR OPTIONS

Our 11" x 14" **Heartland Home Plans™ Color Renderings** are available in a variety of formats. Option 1: An artist's hand-colored rendering of the home as originally designed for the Heartland collection – *front elevation only*. Option 2: The same as option 1, with the addition of a separate black and white rendition of the home's original floor plan. Option 3: A *fully customized* rendering, depicting all custom changes made to the plan. All formats available framed or unframed. Call for pricing.

Framed (#CR). Unframed (#CR).

PASS IT ON TO PROSPECTS

Help prospects remember your homes with the **Heartland Home Plans™ Promotional Handout Artwork**. Camera-ready for easy reproduction, each 8 ½" x 11" master copy features a black and white rendered elevation and floor plan of the Heartland home of your choice, plus your name, address, phone number and company logo.

Just $69 (#PHA).

COUNT THE COST — AND SAVE!

Heartland Home Plans™ Estimator's Material List streamlines the budgeting process with extensive quantity take-offs for each Heartland plan. An available IBM formatted disk version makes it even easier to ensure comparable bids and eliminate cost overruns.

Disk and hard copy set, $50 (#MEW).
Hard copy only, $35 (#MEW).

FORWARD OR REVERSE — IT'S YOUR CHOICE

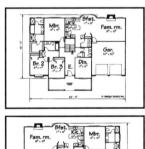

Get the convenience and flexibility of **Right-Reading Reverse Plans** on any Heartland home design. Our CAD-generated reverse versions are available at the same price as originally drafted plans.

Order both the original design and its reverse version at the same time for just an additional $100, or order both for $150 after plan puchase (#RRR).

TAKE THE GUESSWORK OUT OF FRAME WORK

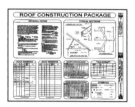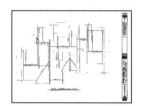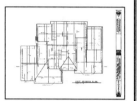

Save time and money with our **Roof Construction Package**. Available for each Design Basics plan, this complete roof framing and dimensional layout includes: 1) Aerial views of the roof showing hips, valleys, ridges, rafters and roof supports. 2) A dimensional plan showing lengths, runs, ridge heights and wall plate heights.

$100 at time of plan purchase.
$150 after plan purchase (#RCP).

UNDERSTAND OUR PLANS — INSIDE AND OUT

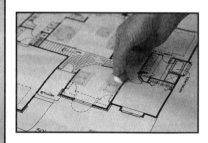

For many home buyers, visualizing the finished home is a challenge. Our **Study Print & Furniture Layout Guide** makes it easy. First, the Study Print provides views of all exterior elevations. Secondly, the Furniture Layout Guide helps them get a "feel" for room sizes, with a ¼" scale floor plan, over 100 reusable furniture pieces and helpful tips on space planning. Specific for any Design Basics plan.

Only $29.95 (#SP).

THE AMENITIES ARE UP TO YOU

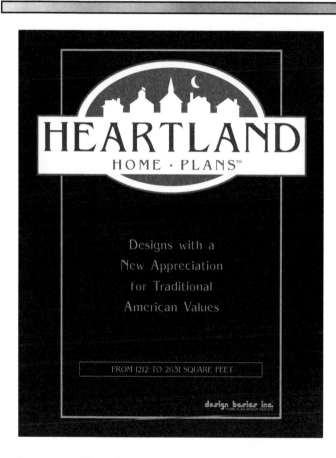

HEARTLAND
HOME · PLANS™

Designs with a
New Appreciation
for Traditional
American Values

FROM 1212 TO 2631 SQUARE FEET

design basics inc.

All 120 plans in the **Heartland Home Plans™ Catalog** reflect down-to-earth, everyday lifestyles with tasteful exteriors and sensibly-designed floorplans. Each design has been evaluated for efficient use of labor and materials. Built-in "extras" are left up to the builder and/or home buyer. And simple rooflines make trussing an easy option!

Just $8.95 (#8005R).

It's the simple things in life that mean the most.

It's a familiar place to call your own.

It's a squeal of laughter

from the backyard.

It's the quiet time together

at the end of the day.

It's a home designed for

what life is really about.

It's our mission:

Design Basics ... Bringing People Home

Gold Seal™ Home Plans

You could say the one-story homes from the Gold Seal™ Home Plans collection were meant to be shown off. These homes feature elevations with attractive touches like brick accents, arched windows and hip roofs for interestingly subtle or immediately charming street appeal. But these one-story homes have much more to offer than eye-catching exteriors. Inside, well thought-out floor plans pay special attention to such necessary things as grocery traffic from garage to the kitchen and convenience between serving and eating areas. A wide variety of thoughtfully designed amenities help enhance specific areas of the home - i.e., a plant shelf in the entry, whirlpool tub in the master bath, entertainment center in the great room or planning desk in the kitchen. Several of the 106 homes in this collection also offer optional den and bedroom layouts to accommodate the different lifestyles of one-story buyers. As a whole, Gold Seal™ one-story designs provide the best of two worlds: thoughtful features and alluring elevations, making owning one of them nothing but pleasurable.

EFFICIENT AND ECONOMICAL

Avery~

- comfortable and economical, this plan is perfect for narrow home sites

- expansive great room with sloped ceiling is warmed by fireplace

- adjacent to volume dining area, well-planned kitchen offers handy snack bar

- master bedroom includes walk-in closet

- optional finished basement plan offers inexpensive living areas including 2 bedrooms, bath, spacious family room and 2 storage areas

- ORDER NO. EL 2568 - PRICE CODE 9

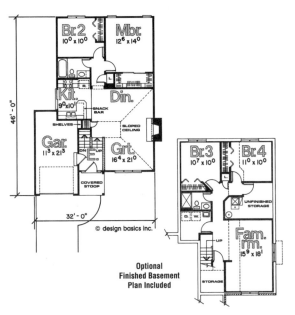

© design basics inc.

Optional Finished Basement Plan Included

Total Square Footage: 962 Dimensions: Width 32' - 0" Depth 46' - 0" Optional Finished Basement 668 Sq. Ft.

OPEN TO ENTERTAIN

Lorain~

- living and dining rooms open for expanded entertaining

- spacious basement area featuring bright windows to the front, well suited for finishing

- kitchen includes snack bar, plant window at sink and lazy Susan

- ORDER NO. EL 1184 - PRICE CODE 9

ALTERNATE ELEVATION INCLUDED AT NO EXTRA COST

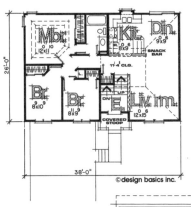

© design basics inc.

Total Square Footage: 975 Dimensions: Width 38' - 0" Depth 26' - 0"

EXPANSIVE ENTRY

Calumet~

- large entry with coat closet on entry level

- volume ceiling for visual expansion

- hallway segregates all bedrooms from primary living areas for privacy

- walk-in closet and private 3/4 bath complete the master suite

- ORDER NO. EL 1129 - PRICE CODE 11

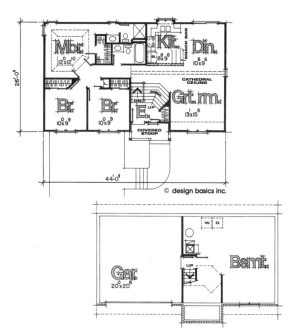

© design basics inc.

Total Square Footage: 1125 Dimensions: Width 44' - 0" Depth 26' - 0"

COZY APPEAL

Dover~

- great room enjoys 10-foot ceiling, window-flanked fireplace, bookcase and easy access to kitchen/dinette

- sunny kitchen/dinette area offers convenient snack bar, wrapping counter and pantry

- cozy secondary bedroom offers privacy to guests or becomes a handy den

- luxurious master bath/dressing area includes whirlpool, roomy walk-in closet and dual lavs

- ORDER NO. EL 2376 - PRICE CODE 12

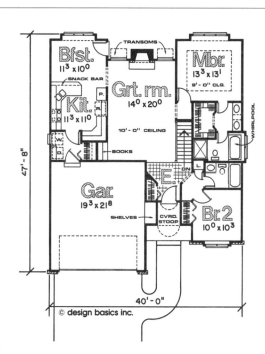

© design basics inc.

Total Square Footage: 1205 Dimensions: Width 40' - 0" Depth 47' - 8"

HOMEY ALLURE

Laurell~

- entry provides immediate access to spacious great room or wood-railed staircase to lower level

- well-designed kitchen, with patio doors leading to covered porch from dinette

- plan offers option to choose formal dining room or create third bedroom

- shaded arbor provides added enjoyment to home

- ORDER NO. EL 2825 - PRICE CODE 12

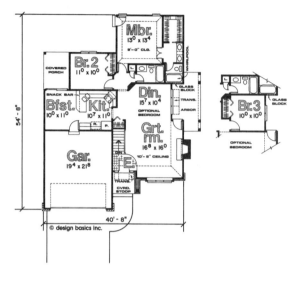

Total Square Footage: 1261 Dimensions: Width 40' - 8" Depth 54' - 8" Optional Bedroom

FOCUS ON FIREPLACE

Logan~

- fireplace centered in great room under cathedral ceiling and surrounded by windows

- dinette with many windows has access to outdoors

- accessible hall linen closet

- laundry area conveniently located near bedrooms

- master dressing area with large vanity, walk-in closet and compartmented stool and shower

- ORDER NO. EL 1551 - PRICE CODE 12

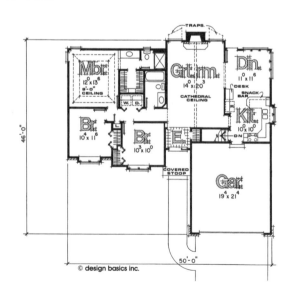

Total Square Footage: 1271 Dimensions: Width 50' - 0" Depth 46' - 0"

INTERESTING ANGLES

Benton~

- volume entry with coat closet, plant ledge and angled staircase

- great room features cathedral ceiling and fireplace framed by windows with elegant quarter-round transoms

- efficient kitchen with corner sink and access to outside

- central hallway angled for maximum privacy

- double doors open into master bedroom with vaulted ceiling, his and her closets, and dressing area with vanity

- Order No. EL 969 - Price Code 13

Total Square Footage: 1305 Dimensions: Width 50' - 0" Depth 50' - 0"

SUNNY GREAT ROOM

Reynolds~

- brick half-wall with palladian arch detailing adds interest to the entrance

- kitchen features snack bar serving the breakfast area and immediate access to garage

- bedrooms are located to the rear of the home for added privacy

- French doors open to the master bath featuring his and her vanities, walk-in closet and compartmented stool

- Order No. EL 3907 - Price Code 13

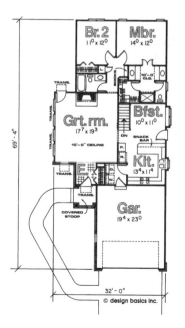

Total Square Footage: 1316 Dimensions: Width 32' - 0" Depth 69' - 4"

ARCHED HIGHLIGHTS

Aspen~

- arched entry highlights brick and siding elevation

- great room with arched windows creates beautiful view from entry

- kitchen features large snack bar and convenient access to spacious utility room

- window at sink overlooks versatile covered area outside

- master suite contains generous walk-in and whirlpool bath with compartmented stool and shower

- ORDER No. EL 3102 - PRICE CODE 13

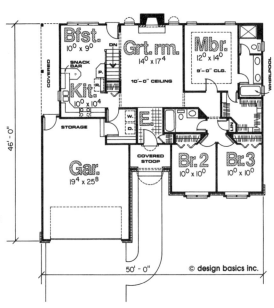

Total Square Footage: 1339 Dimensions: Width 50' - 0" Depth 46' - 0"

NO WASTED SPACE

Mayberry~

- sloped ceiling, and fireplace flanked by windows expands the great room

- kitchen is exceptionally well planned featuring large pantry, 2 lazy Susans and snack bar serving the dinette

- strategically located TV cabinet/entertainment center with affords viewing from great room, dinette or kitchen

- master suite features large walk-in closet and deluxe bath area

- ORDER No. EL 2761 - PRICE CODE 13

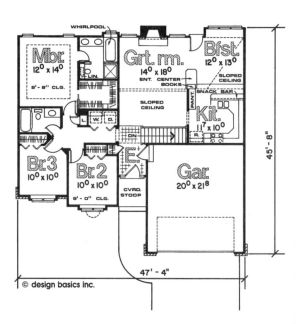

Total Square Footage: 1341 Dimensions: Width 47' - 4" Depth 45 - 8"

OPTIONAL DEN

Kaplin~

- 10-foot-high ceiling in entry and great room

- open staircase for versatile future finished basement

- picture windows with transoms above flank handsome fireplace in great room

- bedroom #3 easily becomes den with French doors off entry

- skylit master dressing/bath area features double vanity and whirlpool on angle under window

- ORDER NO. EL 1963 - PRICE CODE 13

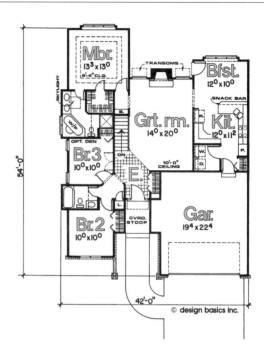

Total Square Footage: 1347 Dimensions: Width 42' - 0" Depth 54' - 0"

ROOM TO EXPAND

Dalton~

- from the entry, only three steps up to the great room with cathedral ceiling, bayed window and fireplace

- vaulted ceiling in dinette and windows on corner angles

- snack bar on island counter plus corner sink and pantry in kitchen

- convenient main floor laundry room with window and soaking sink

- versatile bedroom #3 can become den by adding French doors

- compartmented stool and shower plus walk-in closet in master dressing area

- ORDER NO. EL 2263 - PRICE CODE 13

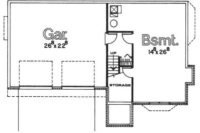

Total Square Footage: 1385 Dimensions: Width 53' - 0" Depth 29' - 8"

Great Room With A View

Westbury~

- covered stoop at entry

- volume great room for visual expansion

- beautiful arches between great room and dinette

- floor-to-ceiling windows in great room

- built-in bookcases

- garage/utility entrance with closet

- master bedroom with vaulted ceiling includes his and her closets, whirlpool tub, skylight and plant ledges plus compartmented stool

- ORDER No. EL 1267 - PRICE CODE 13

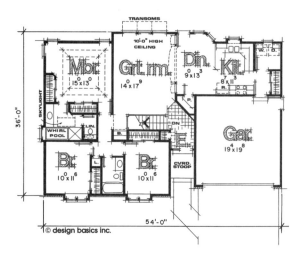

© design basics inc.

Total Square Footage: 1392 Dimensions: Width 54' - 0" Depth 36' - 0"

Prominent Entry

Quimby~

- 12-foot-tall ceiling integrates great room, semi-formal dining room and kitchen

- spacious covered porch accessed from dining room

- arched openings to kitchen with built-in bookcases provide dramatic backdrop for dining area

- master suite features a boxed 9-foot-high ceiling, whirlpool bath and walk-in closet

- space for work bench and sizeable storage area in garage

- ORDER No. EL 3010 - PRICE CODE 14

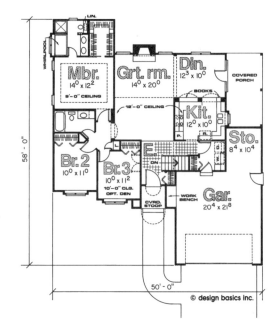

© design basics inc.

Total Square Footage: 1422 Dimensions: Width 50' - 0" Depth 58' - 0"

PRACTICAL APPEAL

Pendleton~

- formal dining room open to large entry with coat closet and wide stairs

- double L-shaped kitchen with boxed window at sink, pantry, and buffet counter

- core hallway opens to large master bedroom with walk-in closet and private bath

- ORDER No. EL 1379 - PRICE CODE 14

ALTERNATE ELEVATION INCLUDED AT NO EXTRA COST

Total Square Footage: 1429 Dimensions: Width 48' - 0" Depth 32' - 0"

MASTER SUITE PRIVACY

Fraser~

- versatility with living room/bedroom option

- snack bar and generous pantry in kitchen adjacent to pleasant dinette

- hanging space and cabinet in convenient laundry room access from garage entry

- master bath features his and her lavs and whirlpool tub under skylight

- ORDER No. EL 2173 - PRICE CODE 14

1-800-947-7526
Order Direct

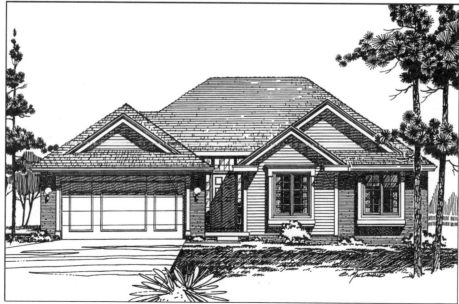

Total Square Footage: 1451 Dimensions: Width 50' - 0" Depth 50' - 0"

QUAINT ACCENTS

Kirby~

- gallery wall in entry has artistic appeal

- breakfast area provides access to rear covered porch

- master suite features access to covered porch, walk-in closet and corner whirlpool

- private den easily converts to optional bedroom

- ORDER NO. EL 3260 - PRICE CODE 14

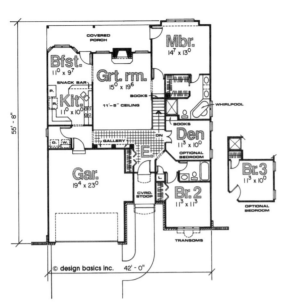

Total Square Footage: 1478 Dimensions: Width 42' - 0" Depth 55' - 8" Optional Bedroom

FRONT PORCH CHARM

Kelsey~

- covered porch adds charm to this ranch home

- sunny great room with 11-foot ceiling open to entry

- bowed breakfast area open to kitchen including island snack bar corner sink and access to back yard

- den with 10-foot-high ceiling and French doors options as a third bedroom

- ORDER NO. EL 3019 - PRICE CODE 14

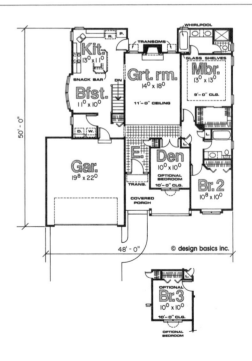

Total Square Footage: 1479 Dimensions: Width 48' - 0" Depth 50' - 0" Optional Bedroom

DEN/BEDROOM OPTIONS

Vinton~

- plan features optional bedroom or private den accessed by French doors

- dinette surrounds you with natural light with its bayed windows and patio door

- sunny master bedroom boasts 9-foot ceiling and built-in bookcase

- master bath has dual vanities, large walk-in closet and oversized whirlpool

- ORDER No. EL 2550 - PRICE CODE 14

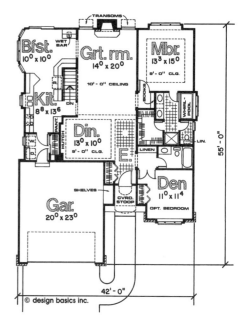

Total Square Footage: 1486 Dimensions: Width 42' - 0" Depth 55' - 0"

COMPACT SOPHISTICATION

Adair~

- tiled entry views spacious great room with window-framed fireplace

- dining area strategic to great room enhances formal or family gatherings

- kitchen/breakfast area designed for enjoyment has utility room nearby

- convenient wet bar/servery serves both kitchen and dining area

- bedroom #3 designed for optional conversion to a den or home office

- luxurious master suite enjoys sunlit whirlpool, dual lav dressing area and roomy walk-in closet

- ORDER No. EL 2300 - PRICE CODE 14

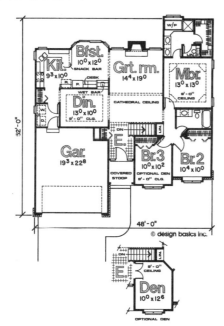

Total Square Footage: 1496 Dimensions: Width 48' - 0" Depth 52' - 0" Optional Den

Generous Entertaining Space

Gifford~

- optional den/bedroom provides design flexibility

- double doors from great room offer privacy from kitchen

- dinette, featuring desk and snack bar also provides convenient access to outdoors

- garage features built-in workbench

- master suite features deluxe bath with sloped ceiling and plant shelves above an open shower

- Order No. EL 2553 - Price Code 14

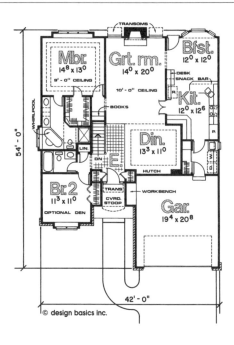

Total Square Footage: 1499 Dimensions: Width 42' - 0" Depth 54' - 0"

Dramatic Entry

Quincy~

- dramatic high entry framed by columns and windows

- expansive great room features sloped ceilings to 11-feet and impressive fireplace surrounded by windows

- complete island kitchen includes lazy Susan, pantry and desk plus adjacent laundry area

- formal ceiling in dining room

- master bath features skylight and walk-in closet

- Order No. EL 679 - Price Code 15

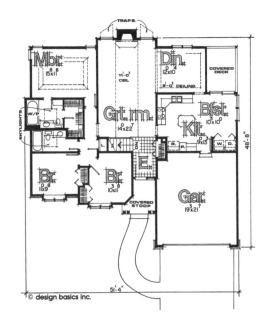

Total Square Footage: 1511 Dimensions: Width 51' - 4" Depth 48' - 8"

WARM AND INVITING

Laramy~

- volume entry adorned with arched transom above door

- kitchen enjoys view to family room through arched opening above sink

- covered porch off breakfast area welcomes relaxation

- cathedral ceiling adds drama to family room with fireplace framed by windows

- spacious walk-in closet, whirlpool under window and dual sink vanity serve master bath

- Order No. EL 3555 - Price Code 15

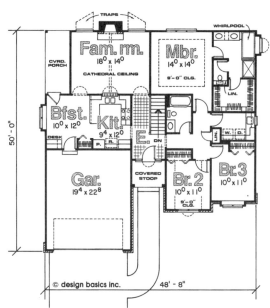

Total Square Footage: 1518 Dimensions: Width 48' - 8" Depth 50' - 0"

CORNER WRAPPING PORCH

Haley~

- entry open to great room with cathedral ceiling and formal dining room with 10-foot-high ceiling

- spacious kitchen features corner sink, built-in bookcase and shares snack bar with breakfast area

- French doors open to master suite with volume ceiling, mirrored doors to walk-in closet and sunny whirlpool bath

- Order No. EL 3127 - Price Code 15

1-800-947-7526
Order Direct

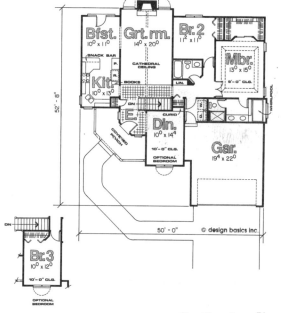

Total Square Footage: 1554 Dimensions: Width 50' - 0" Depth 52' - 8" Optional Bedroom

ANGLED STAIRCASE

Bayley~

- bayed dining area open to great room for expanded entertaining

- large great room with cathedral ceiling features fireplace framed by beautiful windows

- efficient kitchen with pantry, desk and sunny dinette leading to covered patio

- large master suite with his and her closets, whirlpool, 2 lavs with make-up counter and private access to covered deck

- ORDER NO. EL 1770 - PRICE CODE 15

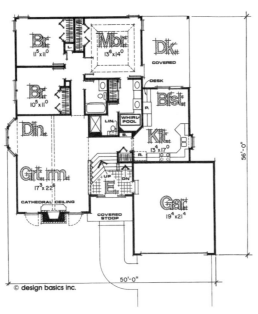

Total Square Footage: 1556 Dimensions: Width 50' - 0" Depth 56' - 0"

FLEXIBLE ARRANGEMENTS

Granite~

- volume entry offers view of great room fireplace

- flexible dining area and great room share 10-foot ceiling

- formal living room converts to optional third bedroom

- breakfast area has built-in desk and access to covered deck or great room

- ORDER NO. EL 2196 - PRICE CODE 15

1-800-947-7526
Order Direct

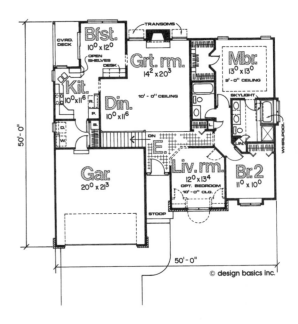

Total Square Footage: 1561 Dimensions: Width 50' - 0" Depth 50' - 0"

EXCITING ANGLED ENTRY

Bradshaw~

- angled entry with covered porch adds interest to this exciting one-story design

- raised-hearth fireplace centered under cathedral ceiling in expansive great room

- well-equipped kitchen with snack bar easily accesses bayed dinette and formal dining room

- private, covered rear patio accessed from dinette

- generous master bedroom offers 9-foot-high boxed ceiling, walk-in closet and whirlpool with window

- ORDER NO. EL 3899 - PRICE CODE 15

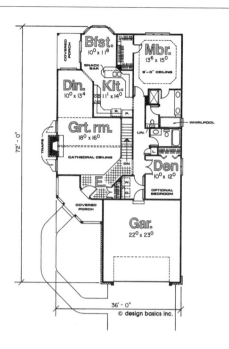

Total Square Footage: 1577 Dimensions: Width 36' - 0" Depth 72' - 0"

© design basics inc.

SCREEN PORCH COMFORT

Tahoe~

- dining room opens to great room, offering view of fireplace

- kitchen features large pantry, planning desk and snack bar

- dinette accesses large, comfortable screen porch

- laundry room is strategically located off kitchen and provides direct access from garage

- French doors access master suite with formal ceiling and pampering bath

- ORDER NO. EL 2537 - PRICE CODE 15

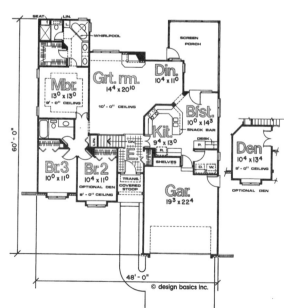

© design basics inc.

Total Square Footage: 1580 Dimensions: Width 48' - 0" Depth 60' - 0" Optional Den

ELEGANT DETAILING

Oakridge~

- striking 10-foot-high entry has plant shelf integrated above closet

- cathedral ceiling and fireplace flanked by trapezoid windows highlight great room

- expansive great room, dining room, sunny kitchen/breakfast area encourage leisure and entertaining pursuits

- compartmented bath features window to flood whirlpool and vanity/makeup area with natural light

- Order No. EL 2324 – Price Code 15

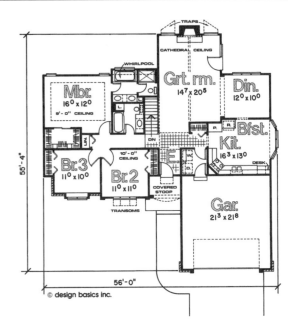

Total Square Footage: 1583 Dimensions: Width 56' - 0" Depth 55' - 4"

OPTIONAL BASEMENT EXPANSION

Stonybrook~

- great room features 10'-0" ceiling and angled see-thru fireplace

- kitchen accommodates boxed window over sink, planning desk and island counter

- master bedroom overlooks private, covered deck

- optional finished basement has plans for additional bedrooms and family room

- Order No. EL 3578 – Price Code 15

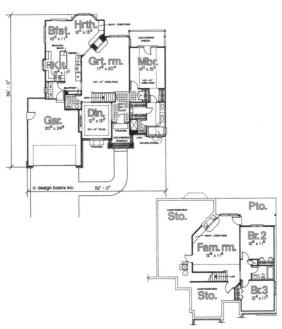

Total Square Footage: 1595 Dimensions: Width 52' - 0" Depth 56' - 0" Optional Finished Basement 790 Sq. Ft.

Private Guest Bedroom

Kirwin~

- formal dining room open to great room

- efficient island kitchen features 2 pantries, lazy Susan, planning desk and sunny breakfast area accessing covered deck

- main floor laundry room conveniently located near bedrooms

- master dressing/bath area complete with double vanity, large walk-in closet and whirlpool tub

- angled hallway offers privacy to guest bedroom and hall bath

- Order No. EL 1017 - Price Code 15

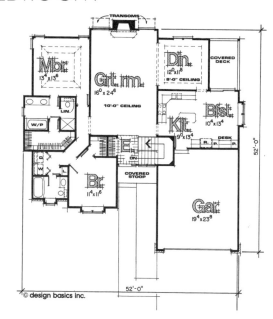

© design basics inc.

Total Square Footage: 1598 Dimensions: Width 52' - 0" Depth 52' - 0"

Family Living

Bradley~

- entry opens to living room with cozy bayed window with a built-in seat

- family room opens to kitchen and has cozy fireplace and cathedral ceiling

- well-designed kitchen/breakfast area with wrapping counters and snack bar

- natural light from a bayed window floods the charming master suite

- Order No. EL 2291 - Price Code 15

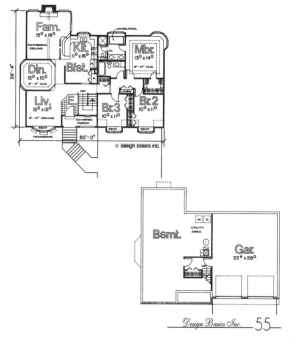

© design basics inc.

Total Square Footage: 1599 Dimensions: Width 50' - 0" Depth 39' - 4"

Roomy Master Suite

Rosebury~

- large volume great room with fireplace flanked by windows to the back seen from entry

- see-thru wet bar between dinette and dining room with formal ceiling

- fully-equipped kitchen with desk, pantry and special window box above sink

- roomy master suite with volume ceiling equipped with special amenities including skylit dressing/bath area with plant shelf, large walk-in closet, double vanity and whirlpool tub

- extra deep garage

- Order No. EL 1767 - Price Code 16

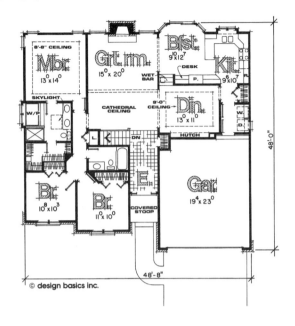

© design basics inc.

ALTERNATE ELEVATION INCLUDED AT NO EXTRA COST

Total Square Footage: 1604 Dimensions: Width 48 - 8" Depth 48' - 0" Optional Alternate Elevation

Designed To Entertain

Sutton~

- U-shaped stairs form beautiful focal point between 10-foot-tall entry and large great room with brick fireplace between built-in entertainment centers

- den with angled French doors off entry is optional bedroom #3

- master suite features nice ceiling detail, sunny whirlpool bath, glass block at shower and generous walk-in closet

- Order No. EL 2923 - Price Code 16

G. McDonald

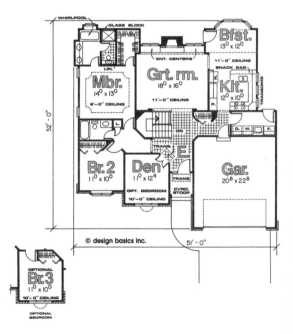

© design basics inc.

Total Square Footage: 1622 Dimensions: Width 51' - 0" Depth 52' - 0" Optional Bedroom

Classic Touches

Leighton~

- great room features cozy fireplace flanked by bright windows

- formal dining room features hutch space and easy access to kitchen area

- gourmet kitchen and bayed dinette includes snack bar, wrapping counters, planning desk and access to outdoors

- secondary bedrooms share bath; bedroom #3 designed as optional den

- master dressing/bath area includes skylight, his and her vanities and corner whirlpool

- ORDER No. EL 2377 - PRICE CODE 16

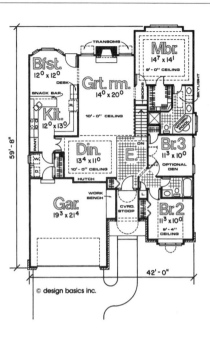

Total Square Footage: 1636 Dimensions: Width 42' - 0" Depth 59' - 8"

Secluded Side Porch

Ithaca~

- covered porch provides a pleasant focal point on this home's front elevation

- great room and dining room are both connected and enhanced by openings that flank a see-thru fireplace and mantle

- kitchen with 2 lazy Susans, pantry and snack bar opens to spacious breakfast area with access to covered side porch

- laundry room is located near bedrooms and hall bath for practicality and convenience

- ORDER No. EL 3915 - PRICE CODE 16

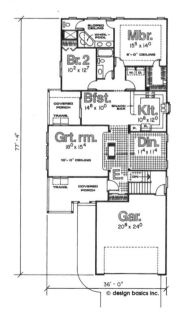

Total Square Footage: 1643 Dimensions: Width 36' - 0" Depth 77' - 4"

Porches Front And Back

Orchard~

- covered front porch with wood railing combines with covered rear porch to expand living space outside

- bright, bayed breakfast area offers access to covered porch

- den with wet bar enhances privacy of master suite or can be converted to optional third bedroom

- Order No. EL 2818 - Price Code 16

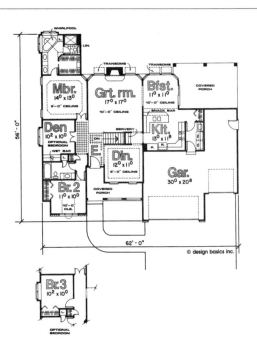

Total Square Footage: 1651 Dimensions: Width 62' - 0" Depth 56' - 0" Optional Bedroom

Bright & Airy Sunroom

Ashley~

- entry captures fantastic views from great room to sun room with arched windows

- peninsula kitchen featuring corner sink and snack bar is open to breakfast area

- sun room offers access to breakfast area, great room and master suite or can option as a lovely dining room

- spacious master suite includes whirlpool bath with dual lavs and walk-in closet

- den off entry has bedroom option

- Order No. EL 2907 - Price Code 16

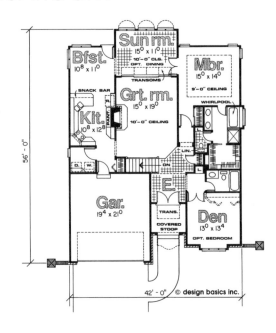

Total Square Footage: 1658 Dimensions: Width 42' - 0" Depth 56' - 0"

BRICK AND STUCCO SHOWCASE

Monterey~

- inviting entry with view into great room is enhanced by arched window and plant shelves above

- fireplace in great room framed by sunny windows with transoms above

- bayed window dining room nestled between great room and superb kitchen/breakfast area

- peaceful master suite enjoys vaulted ceiling, roomy walk-in closet and sunlit master bath with dual lavs and whirlpool

- ORDER No. EL 2290 - PRICE CODE 16

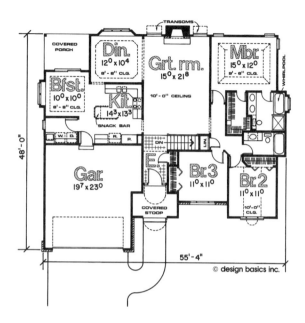

Total Square Footage: 1666 Dimensions: Width 55' - 4" Depth 48' - 0"

© design basics inc.

REAR GARAGE

Montclare~

- arched brick detailing and columns at the covered stoop provide a refined air to the elevation

- island kitchen adjoins spacious breakfast area with access to outdoors

- master suite includes volume of sloped ceiling, skylit dressing area with double vanity, whirlpool tub and walk-in closet

- ORDER No. EL 3889 - PRICE CODE 16

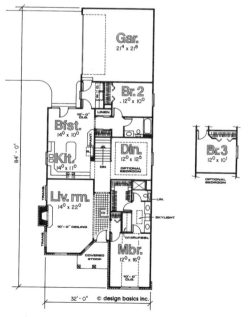

1-800-947-7526
Order Direct

Total Square Footage: 1684 Dimensions: Width 32' - 0" Depth 84' - 0" Optional Bedroom

© design basics inc.

MAGNIFICENT REAR VIEWS

Covington~

- floor-to-ceiling windows in great room viewed from entry

- main floor laundry room strategically located

- master bath includes whirlpool tub, dual vanity and generous walk-in closet

- efficient double-L kitchen with bayed breakfast area to the back

- ORDER NO. EL 1262 - PRICE CODE 16

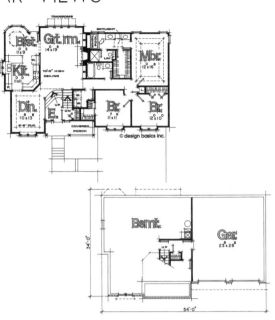

Total Square Footage: 1696 Dimensions: Width 54' - 0" Depth 34' - 0"

SEPARATED SLEEPING

Monte Vista~

- volume dining room with hutch space and elegant arched window open to entry

- expansive great room with 10-foot ceiling offers brick fireplace framed by windows to the back

- kitchen with wrapping counters, snack bar corner sink and pantry

- garage accesses home through conveniently located laundry room

- ORDER NO. 1032 - PRICE CODE 16

1-800-947-7526
Order Direct

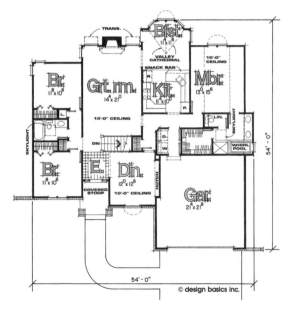

Total Square Footage: 1697 Dimensions: Width 54' - 0" Depth 54' - 0"

OPTIONAL THIRD BEDROOM

Dunbar~

- covered front porch shelters side entry and adds charming appeal

- entry provides an expansive view across great room, which freely connects to formal dining room

- kitchen with snack bar pantry and window sink, adjoins spacious breakfast area with access to outdoors

- roomy master suite includes dressing area with double vanity, corner windows and a walk-in closet

- ORDER NO. EL 3919 - PRICE CODE 16

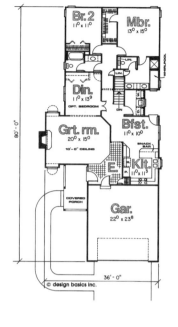

Total Square Footage: 1699   Dimensions: Width 36' - 0" Depth 80' - 0"

DEN/SUNROOM OPTIONS

Waverly~

- kitchen and dinette area with snack bar pantry, and access to outdoors

- two secondary bedrooms convertible to a sun room with French doors from the dinette and an optional den

- secluded master suite features boxed ceiling, skylit dressing area, his and her lavs with knee space between, corner whirlpool tub and roomy walk-in closet

- ORDER NO. EL 2355 - PRICE CODE 17

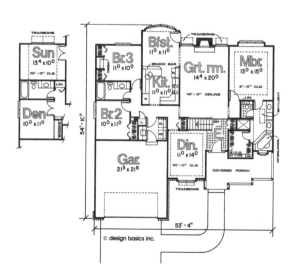

Total Square Footage: 1710   Dimensions: Width 53' - 4" Depth 54' - 10" Optional Den. Sunroom

COOL, SHADED ENTRY

Seville~

- 10-foot-high ceiling for volume in entry, great room and dining room

- dining room open to great room for entertaining options

- open staircase with landing for possible finished basement

- extra length in garage for storage

- angled whirlpool, double vanity and walk-in closet for master dressing area

- ORDER NO. EL 2212 – PRICE CODE 17

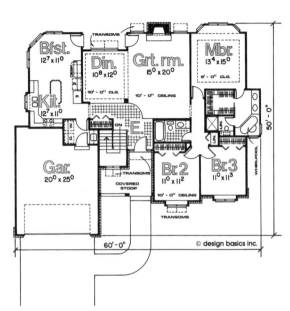

Total Square Footage: 1735 Dimensions: Width 60' - 0" Depth 50' - 0"

COZY HEARTH ROOM

Bennett~

- arched windows and volume ceiling in dining room capture the eye

- hearth area has bayed windows and shares 3-sided fireplace

- master suite enhanced by large walk-in closet and whirlpool tub

- two secondary bedrooms in separate wing from master suite for added privacy

- ORDER NO. EL 3577 – PRICE CODE 17

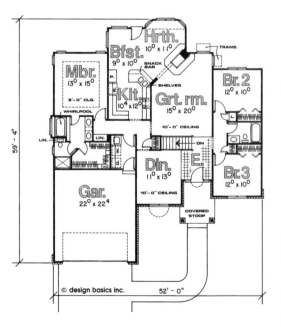

Total Square Footage: 1782 Dimensions: Width 52' - 0" Depth 59' - 4"

Street Appeal

Ogden~

- great room explodes into view with 10'-9" ceiling and lovely windows framing raised hearth fireplace

- volume ceiling and charming windows illuminate formal dining room

- open kitchen includes island cooktop and opening above sink for view of dining room

- bedroom #3 easily converts into den accessed from entry

- Order No. 3298 - Price Code 17

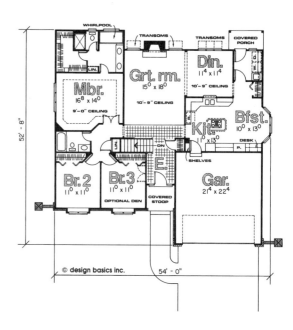

Total Square Footage: 1793 Dimensions: Width 54' - 0" Depth 52' - 8"

Entertain Inside And Out

Charleston~

- dining room has 10'-0" ceiling and French doors to kitchen/hearth room

- volume ceiling adds spaciousness to great room

- kitchen offers snack bar and views entertainment wall

- fireplace and windows brighten hearth room

- screen porch features snack counter

- dual sink vanity and sunny whirlpool tub capture romance in master bedroom

- bedroom #2 serves as an optional den

- Order No. EL 3587 - Price Code 17

Total Square Footage: 1796 Dimensions: Width 58' - 0" Depth 58' - 0"

Appealing Arches

Grayson~

- 10-foot entry has formal views of volume dining room and great room featuring brick fireplace and arched windows

- sunny breakfast room has atrium door to back yard

- garage with built-in shelves accesses home through efficient laundry room

- separate bedroom wings provide optimum privacy

- private master suite includes whirlpool bath with sloped ceiling, plant shelf above dual lavs and large walk-in closet

- Order No. EL 3006 - Price Code 18

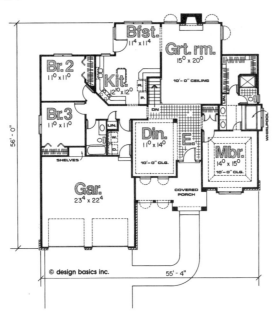

Total Square Footage: 1806 Dimensions: Width 55' - 4" Depth 56' - 0"

Bright, Bayed Great Room

Bancroft~

- 10-foot ceilings through entry, great room and staircase

- roomy kitchen with pantry, 2 lazy Susans and snack bar shares see-thru fireplace with great room

- wet bar/servery between dinette and great room

- master bath has walk-in closet, his and her vanities and corner whirlpool tub with windows above

- Hollywood bath for secondary bedrooms

- Order No. EL 1559 - Price Code 18

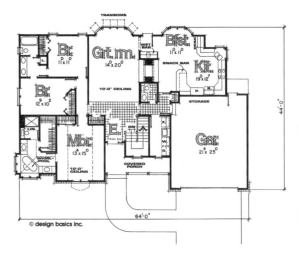

Total Square Footage: 1808 Dimensions: Width 64' - 0" Depth 44' - 0"

SPIRITED CHARM

Winfield~

- special detailing allows a welcoming, yet sophisticated feel to the elevation

- great room is graced by a palladian arch window and raised-hearth fireplace

- interesting angles and decorative column help define border between great room and formal dining room

- kitchen has generous counter space, pantry, snack bar and plenty of natural light

- deluxe master suite features built-in bookcase, his and her vanities, whirlpool tub and walk-in closet

- ORDER NO. EL 3887 - PRICE CODE 18

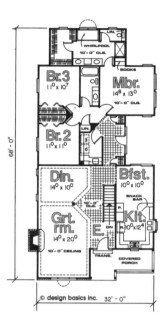

Total Square Footage: 1821 Dimensions: Width 32' - 0" Depth 68' - 0"

GOURMET KITCHEN

Shawnee~

- kitchen/dinette area includes bayed eating area, wrapping counters, desk, island and wet bar/servery for entertaining ease

- impactful 10-foot-high entry

- laundry/mud room with sink and extra counter space

- bedroom #2 can be utilized as an optional den

- master suite enjoys decorative boxed ceiling and elegant windows to the rear, dual lavs, walk-in closet, whirlpool and cedar-lined window seat for storage

- ORDER NO. EL 2461 - PRICE CODE 18

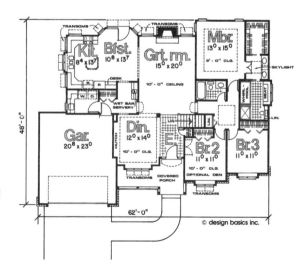

Total Square Footage: 1850 Dimensions: Width 62' - 0" Depth 48' - 0"

KITCHEN - GARAGE CONVENIENCE

Webber~

- entry framed by sidelights and detailed trim adds character

- inside, entry views elegant dining room and spacious great room

- French doors access dining room from kitchen which features planning desk, pantry and corner sink with two windows

- laundry, with space for soaking sink, located near bedrooms

- ORDER No. EL 3894 - PRICE CODE 18

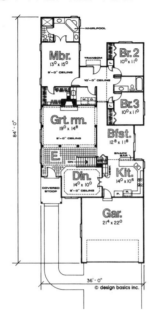

Total Square Footage: 1864 Dimensions: Width 36' - 0" Depth 84' - 0"

INVITING FIREPLACE

Tatum~

- generous 11'-11" ceiling in great room invites guests inside

- dining room has views to the back through picturesque windows

- breakfast area with planning desk connects kitchen and dining room

- back porch is great place to relax

- secluded bedroom wing

- French doors add elegance to master bath equipped with leisurely whirlpool tub and double vanity

- ORDER No. EL 3299 - PRICE CODE 18

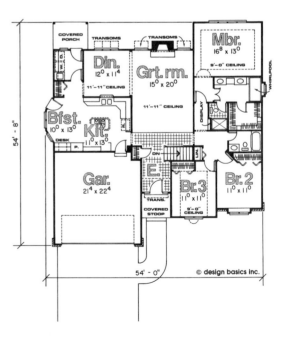

Total Square Footage: 1873 Dimensions: Width 54' - 0" Depth 54' - 8"

EXPANSIVE VIEWS FROM ENTRY

Stockville~

- entrance is granted privacy with spacious front courtyard

- impactful entry offers views through open dining room, to sizeable great room with raised-hearth fireplace

- kitchen adjoins breakfast area with direct access to covered porch

- master suite offers skylit dressing area with double vanity and walk-in closet

- ORDER No. EL 3891 - PRICE CODE 18

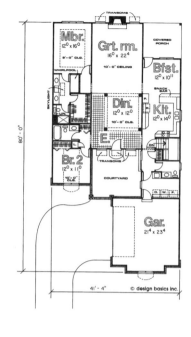

Total Square Footage: 1883 Dimensions: Width 41' - 4" Depth 80' - 0"

SEE-THROUGH FIREPLACE

Thomasville~

- successive tiers layer the front elevation, providing visual intrigue

- open formal dining room features special ceiling details and a see-thru fireplace

- great room features a flush-hearth fireplace, expansive views to the rear and open access to the dinette

- master bath includes walk-in closet, whirlpool and double vanity under a sloped ceiling

- ORDER No. EL 3879 - PRICE CODE 18

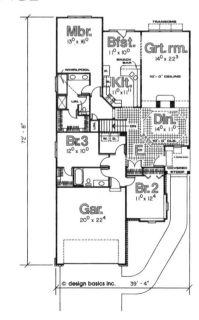

Total Square Footage: 1885 Dimensions: Width 39' - 4" Depth 72' - 8"

MAJESTIC WINDOWS

Hawthorne~

- integrated design of gathering room, dinette and kitchen for family living

- master dressing area with angled lavs, make-up counter and walk-in closet

- optional finished basement designed for independent living, with kitchen, bath and private access

- ORDER NO. EL 2799 - PRICE CODE 18

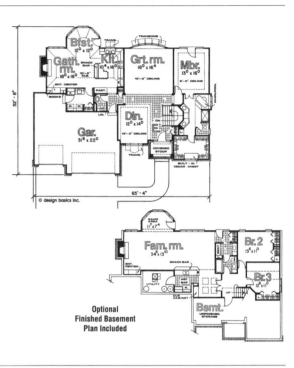

Optional
Finished Basement
Plan Included

Total Square Footage: 1887 Dimensions: Width 65' - 4" Depth 52' - 8" Optional Finished Basement 1338 Sq. Ft.

ROOM TO RELAX

Sinclair~

- beautiful arched dining room window and detailed ceiling to 12 feet high

- see-thru fireplace seen from entry

- add French doors to bedroom adjacent to great room for optional den, remove closet for built-in bookcase

- master bath area with skylight, whirlpool, his and her vanity and walk-in closet

- ORDER NO. EL 1748 - PRICE CODE 19

1-800-947-7526
Order Direct

ALTERNATE ELEVATION INCLUDED AT NO EXTRA COST

Total Square Footage: 1911 Dimensions: Width 56' - 0" Depth 58' - 0" Optional Alternate Elevation

OPEN DESIGN

Surrey~

- entry with 10-foot ceiling views open dining room with tapered columns

- gourmet kitchen includes island, pantry and wet bar/servery

- great room enjoys a warm fireplace flanked by large windows

- pampering master bath with his and her vanities, whirlpool, linen cabinet, special shower and walk-in closet

- ORDER NO. EL 2384 - PRICE CODE 19

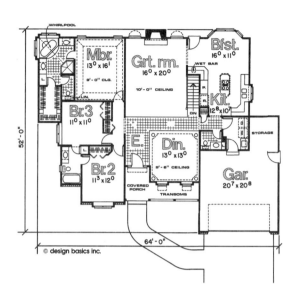

Total Square Footage: 1948 Dimensions: Width 64' - 0" Depth 52' - 0"

ELEGANT ANGLES

Glenmorrie~

- dining room displays elegance of 10'-0" ceiling

- volume great room offers plenty of space and light for gathering

- hearth room off the kitchen highlighted with warm fireplace between glass

- secluded bedroom wing

- master bedroom boasts boxed ceiling

- walk-in closet and whirlpool under sloped ceiling are features in master suite

- corner closet in roomy laundry

- ORDER NO. EL 3553 - PRICE CODE 19

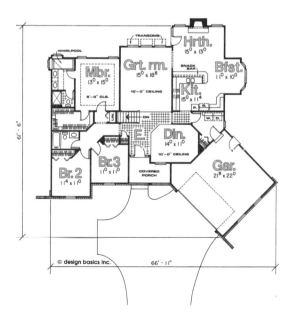

Total Square Footage: 1960 Dimensions: Width 66' - 11" Depth 61' - 6"

SECLUDED FAMILY ROOM

Cedardale~

- dramatic stairs with dome ceiling above are unique features

- island with cooktop range, roomy pantry and desk highlight kitchen/dinette area

- family room has inviting brick fireplace and spacious windows to back

- volume ceiling and arched transom window complement master bedroom

- master bath includes 10' - 4" ceiling, oval whirlpool tub and walk-in closet

- laundry room is located close to bedrooms and offers sunny window

- ORDER No. EL 3276 - PRICE CODE 19

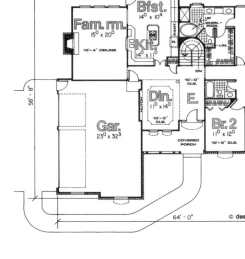

Total Square Footage: 1973 Dimensions: Width 64' - 0" Depth 58' - 8"

FRONT AND SIDE COVERED PORCHES

Jonesville~

- dramatic formal dining room open to 10-foot-tall entry

- family room open to kitchen and breakfast area provides great atmosphere for informal gatherings

- breakfast area with 2 pantries and built-in desk complements island kitchen

- laundry has access to covered porch

- French doors open to master suite, enhanced by private back yard access and whirlpool bath with spacious closet and dual lavs

- ORDER No. EL 3031 - PRICE CODE 19

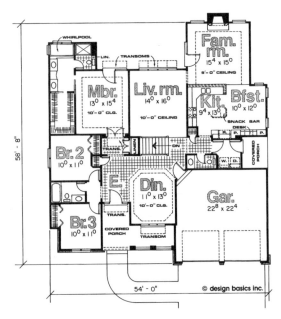

Total Square Footage: 1978 Dimensions: Width 54' - 0" Depth 58' - 8"

THREE CAR TANDEM

Mansfield~

- formal dining room with hutch space and tiered ceiling up to 11 feet high

- combination mud/laundry room for easy access from garage

- tandem 3-car drive-through garage

- gorgeous fireplace surrounded by windows in great room with built-in bookcase and 10-foot ceiling

- skylit master bath with whirlpool, his and her vanities and plant ledge

- living room with volume ceiling can become third bedroom

- Order No. EL 1539 - Price Code 19

Total Square Footage: 1996 Dimensions: Width 64' - 0" Depth 50' - 0"

ROMANTIC APPEAL

Summerwood~

- assets in ideal great room include 3-sided see-thru fireplace, entertainment center and bookcases

- kitchen features snack bar, pantry and ample counter space

- window seat framed by closets enhances bedroom #2; bedroom #3 can be converted to an optional den

- Order No. EL 2361 - Price Code 20

1-800-947-7526
Order Direct

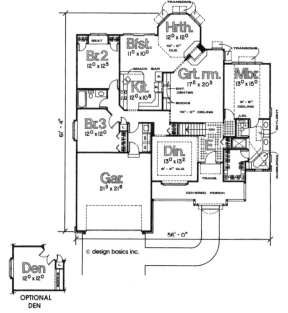

Total Square Footage: 2015 Dimensions: Width 56' - 0" Depth 61' - 4" Optional Den

ROMANTIC COURTYARD

Tecumseh~

- brick wing walls enhance the privacy of this home's romantic front courtyard

- entry opens to dramatic views of dining room and great room beyond

- kitchen with snack bar, pantry and plenty of counter space adjoins breakfast area with direct access to covered rear porch

- master bedroom with walk-in closet, opens to bath area with corner whirlpool and separate vanities

- ORDER NO. EL 3892 – PRICE CODE 20

Total Square Footage: 2035 Dimensions: Width 41' - 4" Depth 94' - 0"

INTRIGUING LAYOUT

Atwood~

- plan allows den off entry to be converted to optional third bedroom

- tall windows, fireplace and 10-foot ceiling adds sophistication to great room

- French doors open to airy dinette/kitchen area with access to outside

- accessed by French doors, the master bedroom features large walk-in closet

- ORDER NO. EL 2843 – PRICE CODE 20

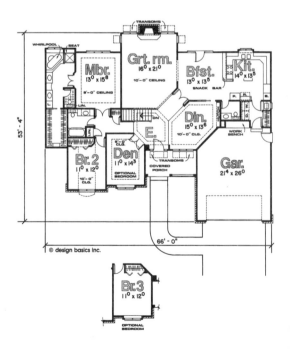

Total Square Footage: 2047 Dimensions: Width 66' - 0" Depth 53' - 4" Optional Bedroom

UNIVERSALLY DESIGNED

Foxboro~

- universally designed home

- sizeable breakfast area shines with bayed windows and access to screen porch

- master suite features bayed window, roomy closet, dressing area, dual lavs, whirlpool bath and oversized shower

- ORDER No. EL 3139 - PRICE CODE 20

Total Square Footage: 2053 Dimensions: Width 67' - 8" Depth 58' - 0" Optional Elevator Location

COVERED VERANDA

Plainview~

- elegant covered veranda at entry

- 3-sided fireplace serves gathering areas

- den becomes third bedroom with optional door location

- master suite with private covered deck, dressing area with whirlpool and large walk-in closet

- ORDER No. EL 2222 - PRICE CODE 20

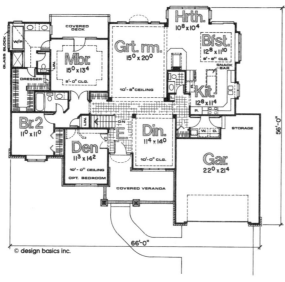

Total Square Footage: 2068 Dimensions: Width 66' - 0" Depth 56' - 0"

Design Basics Inc. 73

FAMILY-FRIENDLY SPACE

Richardson~

- gourmet kitchen features wrapping cabinets, island, double oven and pantry

- hearth room with entertainment center shares 3-sided fireplace with great room

- optional finished basement plan shows secondary bedrooms, informal living area and plenty of storage

- Order No. EL 3303 - Price Code 20

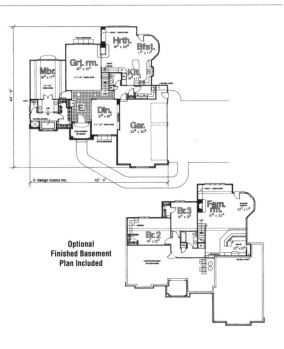

Optional Finished Basement Plan Included

Total Square Footage: 2083 Dimensions: Width 63' - 4" Depth 64' - 8" Optional Finished Basement 1403 Sq. Ft..

EYE-CATCHING ELEVATION

Pickford~

- 10-foot ceiling in great room with raised hearth fireplace and windows with arched transoms above

- formal dining room close to great room and kitchen area affords entertaining ease

- island kitchen and bayed dinette with outside access features desk and pantry

- comfortable secondary bedrooms are apart from private master suite

- master suite includes boxed ceiling, walk-in closet, his and her vanities with knee space and whirlpool tub

- Order No. EL 2454 - Price Code 20

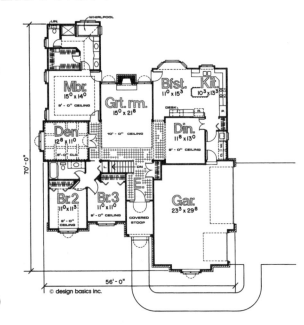

Total Square Footage: 2093 Dimensions: Width 56' - 0" Depth 70' - 0"

CONVENIENT GARAGE

Galloway~

- ceiling details enhance formal dining room

- formal living room has view of screen porch through spacious windows

- family room is warmed by fireplace and provides access to screen porch

- breakfast/kitchen area boasts broom closet, snack bar pantry and lazy Susans

- master suite features large walk-in closet, dual lavs and whirlpool bath

- secondary bedrooms share convenient hall bath

- ORDER NO. EL 3196 - PRICE CODE 21

Total Square Footage: 2120 Dimensions: Width 58' - 0" Depth 68' - 0"

GENEROUS PORCHES

Concorde~

- oak entry views elegant living room with French doors to covered patio

- raised hearth fireplace warms secluded family room

- sunny whirlpool and walk-in closet complete master suite

- secondary bedrooms in secluded wing afford privacy for master suite

- covered patio enhanced with tapered columns

- ORDER NO. EL 3597 - PRICE CODE 21

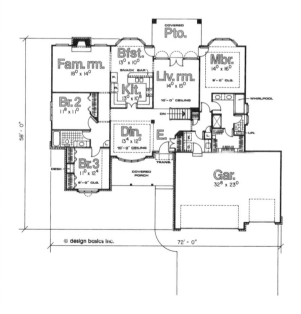

Total Square Footage: 2132 Dimensions: Width 72' - 0" Depth 58' - 0"

VISUALLY OPEN

Newman~

- entry views volume great room with fireplace flanked by windows

- island kitchen with snack bar desk and walk-in pantry

- 3-car garage with extra storage space accesses home through mud/laundry room

- double doors lead to master bedroom with tiered ceiling and access to covered deck

- romantic master bath with whirlpool, double vanity and walk-in closet

- ORDER NO. EL 1689 - PRICE CODE 21

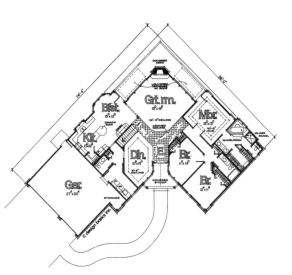

Total Square Footage: 2133 Dimensions: Width 58' - 0" Depth 74' - 4"

SUNNY BREAKFASTS

Gregory~

- formal entry views great room and dining room with 10'-4" ceilings

- angled breakfast area with octagon ceiling detail is accessible to kitchen and dining room

- peninsula kitchen features snack bar 2 pantries and buffet

- separated dressing area, whirlpool bath and walk-in closet complement this master suite

- ORDER NO. EL 3145 - PRICE CODE 21

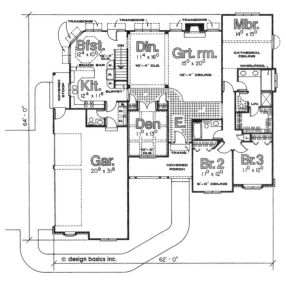

Total Square Footage: 2141 Dimensions: Width 62' - 0" Depth 64' - 0"

Tasteful Detailing

Roxbury~

- long views through great room create sense of spaciousness

- formal dining room with hutch space and 12-foot-high ceiling

- island kitchen includes 42" pantry, planning desk and snack bar

- see-thru fireplace serves kitchen, breakfast area, and volume great room

- front bedroom with window seat, 10-foot ceiling and pocket door to bath easily converts to den

- private master suite bath area with plant shelf and step-up whirlpool

- Order No. EL 2848 - Price Code 21

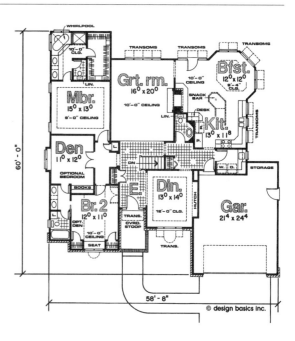

Total Square Footage: 2148 Dimensions: Width 58' - 8" Depth 60' - 0"

Comfortable Family Room

Essex~

- open entry views formal rooms

- service doors to close off kitchen from entry and dining room

- open staircase for future finished basement

- private master suite with walk-in closet, double vanity and whirlpool under windows

- Order No. EL 2213 - Price Code 21

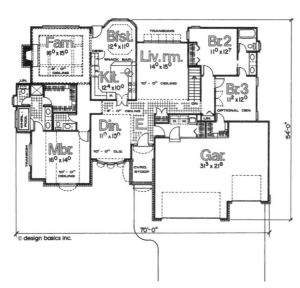

Total Square Footage: 2149 Dimensions: Width 70' - 0" Depth 54' - 0"

Views To The Rear

Greensboro~

- formal living and dining rooms flanking entry give ease in entertaining

- impressive great room with 11-foot ceiling and picture/awning windows framing a raised-hearth fireplace

- attractive kitchen/dinette area with island, desk, wrapping counters, walk-in pantry and access to covered patio

- growing families or empty nesters have the option of converting two bedrooms to other uses

- ORDER No. EL 2326 - PRICE CODE 21

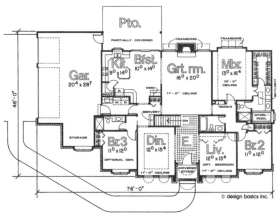

Total Square Footage: 2172 Dimensions: Width 76' - 0" Depth 46' - 0"

Stately Gables

Wrenwood~

- bright 12-foot-tall entry views large great room with entertainment center, brick fireplace and direct access to dining room and kitchen

- utility corridor has laundry room to one side and computer center to the other

- 3-car garage has sunlit shop area

- bedroom #3 offers versatile den option

- master suite has spacious walk-in closet, lavish whirlpool bath and 10-foot ceiling in bedroom

- ORDER No. EL 3005 - PRICE CODE 21

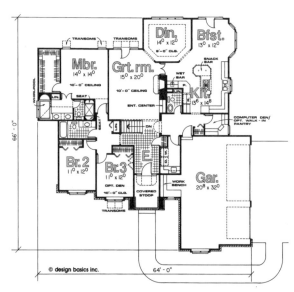

Total Square Footage: 2186 Dimensions: Width 64' - 0" Depth 66' - 0"

REPEATING ARCHES

Brentwood~

- multiple arched windows accentuate impressive great room

- snack bar and island counter equip kitchen and breakfast area

- French doors reveal master suite with walk-in closet, oval whirlpool and double sink vanity

- bedroom #2 easily converted to a den

- ORDER NO. EL 3598 - PRICE CODE 21

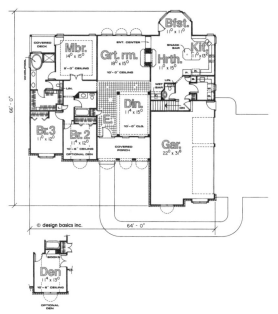

Total Square Footage: 2187 Dimensions: Width 64' - 0" Depth 66' - 0" Optional Den

SPRAWLING ENTRY

Alvarado~

- grand entry hall has views to formal dining room, great room and den with bedroom option

- volume great room has fireplace and cased opening to breakfast area with back yard access

- curio cabinet and 2 pantries highlight peninsula kitchen

- master suite offers private covered porch and whirlpool bath

- ORDER NO. EL 3128 - PRICE CODE 21

1-800-947-7526
Order Direct

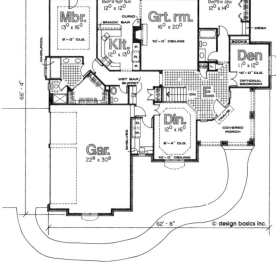

Total Square Footage: 2199 Dimensions: Width 62' - 8" Depth 66' - 4"

BEAUTIFULLY BALANCED

Osage~

- grand entry centers on formal great room with 10'-8" ceiling, brick fireplace and arched windows

- gourmet kitchen features double oven, large pantry and pass-thru buffet

- beautifully vaulted ceiling in breakfast area enhances informal meals

- symmetry continues in the master suite with French doors between his and her walk-in closets, centering on the vanity and cathedral ceiling in the elegant bath

- unique curved stairway to basement

- ORDER NO. EL 2934 - PRICE CODE 22

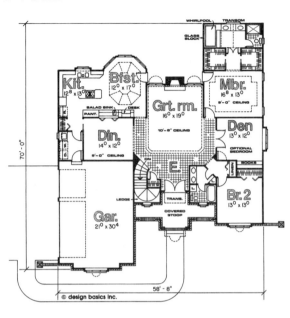

Total Square Footage: 2233 Dimensions: Width 58' - 8" Depth 70' - 0"

SOPHISTICATED CHARM

Beaumont~

- floor-to-ceiling windows in great room seen from entry

- see-thru fireplace centered under cathedral ceiling in great room

- optional den or bedroom with French doors

- master bath includes double vanity, step-up whirlpool, large walk-in closet and glass block wall at shower

- ORDER NO. EL 1388 - PRICE CODE 22

1-800-947-7526
Order Direct

Total Square Footage: 2254 Dimensions: Width 64' - 0" Depth 69' - 4"

EXPANSIVE ELEVATION

Blanchard~

- entry presents bowed dining room

- volume 11'-0" ceiling gives elegance to living room

- walk-in pantry and angled island counter in kitchen

- octagonal breakfast area surrounded with gorgeous views

- casual family room easily accesses back porch

- master suite has two pairs of French doors; one leading to a large walk-in closet and the other revealing a romantic bayed whirlpool tub

• ORDER NO. EL 3523 - PRICE CODE 22

Total Square Footage: 2274 Dimensions: Width 80' - 8" Depth 65' - 7"

EXQUISITE MASTER SUITE

Aberdeen~

- expansive entry views den with French doors and open dining room

- gourmet kitchen and bayed breakfast area features wet bar/servery, wrapping counters and desk

- secluded secondary bedrooms enhanced by easy access to compartmented bath with two lavs

- master suite has his/her closets and built-in dresser/entertainment center

• ORDER NO. EL 2321- PRICE CODE 22

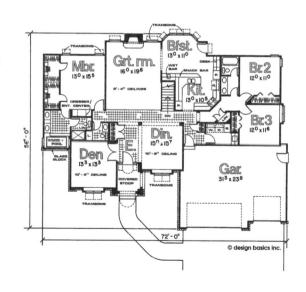

ALTERNATE ELEVATION INCLUDED AT NO EXTRA COST

Total Square Footage: 2276 Dimensions: Width 72' - 0" Depth 56' - 0" Optional Alternate Elevation

WELL-PLANNED KITCHEN

Montgomery~

- great room highlighted by pass thru wet bar/buffet

- kitchen features walk-in pantry and wrapping island snack bar

- ample laundry room has desirable access to covered service porch

- corridor design offers privacy between master suite and secondary bedrooms

- his and her walk-in closets, large dressing area and separate shower and whirlpool space in bath produce stylish master suite

- ORDER NO. EL 3058 – PRICE CODE 23

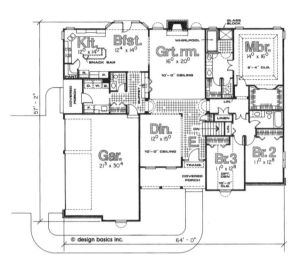

Total Square Footage: 2311 Dimensions: Width 64' - 0" Depth 57' - 2"

PLENTY OF OPTIONS

Fairway~

- 3-sided fireplace joins great and hearth rooms together in perfect harmony

- charming sitting room and spacious walk-in closet in master bedroom

- optional finished lower level plan (included) features see-thru fireplace, kitchenette and entertainment center

- ORDER NO. EL 2651 – PRICE CODE 23

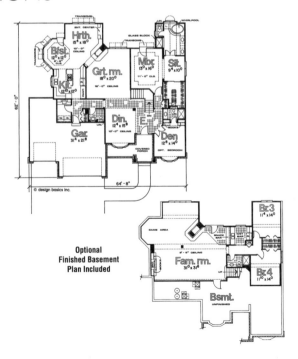

Optional Finished Basement Plan Included

Total Square Footage: 2317 Dimensions: Width 64' - 8" Depth 62' - 0" Optional Finished Basement 1475 Sq. Ft.

Pampering Amenities

Harcourt~

- 10-foot-high entry surveys den, dining room and great room

- lovely den with double doors, spider-beam ceiling, bookcases and bathroom access could easily convert to a bedroom

- kitchen/dinette has sunny bayed area, island and pantry

- spacious hearth room with window-flanked fireplace, wet bar entertainment center and door to outside

- master bedroom features vaulted ceiling, his and her closets and door to outside

- Order No. EL 2459 - Price Code 23

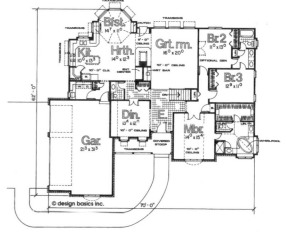

Total Square Footage: 2335 Dimensions: Width 68' - 0" Depth 58' - 8" Optional Bedroom

Showy Breakfast Area

Melbourne~

- spectacular 3-sided fireplace for great room and hearth room

- formal ceiling and boxed windows accent dining room

- open kitchen with island counter and walk-in corner pantry

- luxurious master dressing area with his and her vanities, angled oval whirlpool and large walk-in closet

- Order No. EL 2192 - Price Code 23

Total Square Footage: 2355 Dimensions: Width 70' - 0" Depth 62' - 0"

EMBELLISHED WITH BRICK

Tangent~

- living room offers 10'-0" ceiling and opts as fourth bedroom

- bowed windows in breakfast area and snack bar peninsula in kitchen

- combined great room, kitchen and breakfast area convenient for family

- 10'-0" ceiling in master bedroom with access to private deck

- master bath highlights include corner whirlpool tub, his and her vanities and large walk-in closet

- secondary bedrooms in separate wing for added privacy

- ORDER NO. EL 3524 - PRICE CODE 23

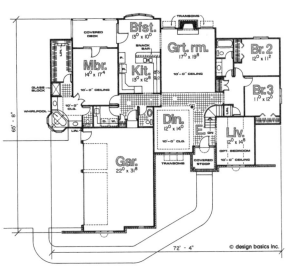

Total Square Footage: 2366 Dimensions: Width 72' - 4" Depth 65' - 8"

SHADED ENTERTAINING

Nottsbury~

- well designed covered stoop ties together this attractive front elevation

- living room with 11-foot ceiling and French doors leads to covered veranda

- covered porch off master bedroom offers excellent private retreat outdoors

- ORDER NO. EL 3514 - PRICE CODE 23

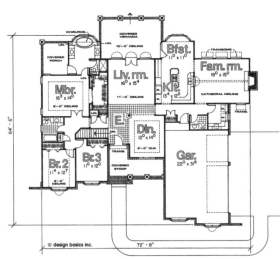

Total Square Footage: 2399 Dimensions: Width 72' - 8" Depth 64' - 6"

DRAMATIC DOMES

Evanston~

- dramatic domed ceilings repeated in stairwell, dinette and master bath

- dining room defined by columns seen from entry

- beautiful great room with repetitive arched windows

- see-thru fireplace creates hearth room on kitchen side

- optional den or bedroom up front with direct access to bath

- large master suite includes open shower, special lighting, large walk-in closet and stylish whirlpool

- ORDER NO. EL 1232 - PRICE CODE 24

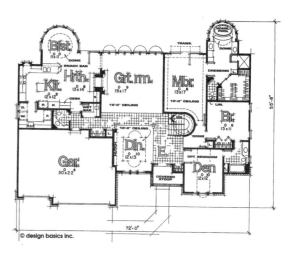

Total Square Footage: 2422 Dimensions: Width 72' - 0" Depth 55' - 8"

STATELY DETAILS

Comstock~

- open great room features wet bar, fireplace and tall windows allowing natural light

- wide kitchen features island, 2 pantries and easy laundry access

- double doors open to master suite with French doors leading to master bath and covered porch

- master bath with whirlpool, dual lavs, plant shelves and large walk-in closet

- ORDER NO. EL 2778 - PRICE CODE 24

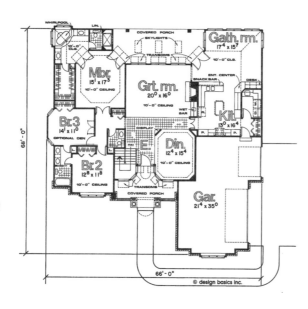

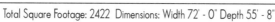

Total Square Footage: 2456 Dimensions: Width 66' - 0" Depth 68' - 0"

LUXURY THROUGHOUT

Hillsboro~

- bedroom #2 with optional French doors can be utilized as a den

- gigantic hearth room with snack bar and door to roomy covered veranda

- entertainment-sized kitchen and sunny dinette also ideal for family gathering

- pampering master suite includes doors to outside, boxed ceiling, French doors to dressing area and luxurious bath with whirlpool, dual lavs and make-up counter

- ORDER NO. EL 2472 - PRICE CODE 24

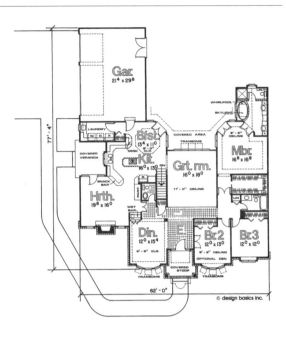

Total Square Footage: 2470 Dimensions: Width 62' - 0" Depth 77' - 4"

COMFORTABLE LIVING

Hawkesbury~

- entry views formal dining room and living room beyond

- gazebo dinette open to family room

- staircase open for future finished basement

- versatile den can become fourth bedroom

- bedroom #3 easily converts to sitting area for master bedroom

- luxurious dressing area in master suite with his and her vanities, large walk-in closet and oval whirlpool below windows

- ORDER NO. EL 2206 - PRICE CODE 24

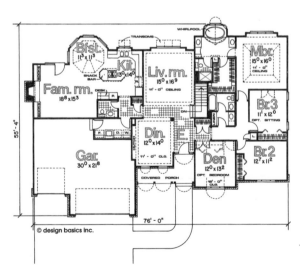

Total Square Footage: 2498 Dimensions: Width 76' - 0" Depth 55' - 4"

IMPRESSIVE, IMPACTFUL

Hallmark~

- see-thru fireplace and French doors to back highlight living and dining rooms

- screened in porch located off sunny breakfast area

- kitchen provides snack bar, island counter, easy access to dining room and cathedral ceiling stretching to gathering room

- master bedroom features 10'-0" boxed ceiling and private access to the back

- French doors, matching vanities, walk-in closet and stylish oval whirlpool illuminate master bath

- ORDER No. EL 3535 - PRICE CODE 25

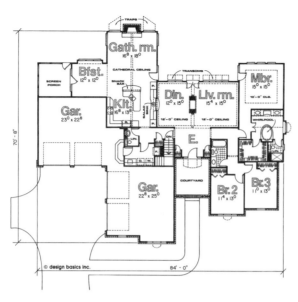

© design basics inc.

Total Square Footage: 2504 Dimensions: Width 84' - 0" Depth 70' - 8"

GOLF COURSE VIEWS

Lawrence~

- impressive 12" tapered columns define formal dining room with 10-foot ceiling

- domed ceiling above curved landing for stairs to basement

- French doors open into den with twin curio cabinets or convert den to third bedroom with built-in desk

- curved wall in sumptuous master bedroom with vaulted ceiling

- ORDER No. EL 2652 - PRICE CODE 25

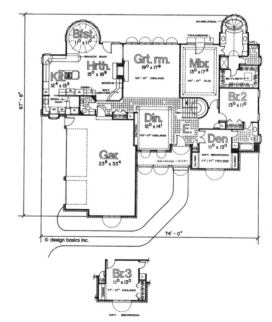

© design basics inc.

Total Square Footage: 2512 Dimensions: Width 74' - 0" Depth 67' - 8" Optional Bedroom

GRAND FRONT PORCH

Ascott~

- grand front porch creates majestic elevation

- living room and bedroom #2/optional den each have 10-foot ceilings

- island kitchen features abundant pantries, lazy Susan and snack bar

- spacious laundry/mud room off kitchen has convenient dual access

- private bedroom wing offers 2 secondary bedrooms and luxurious master suite featuring spacious walk-in closet with built-in dressers, and private access to back yard

- ORDER NO. EL 3057 - PRICE CODE 25

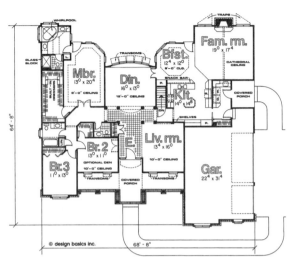

Total Square Footage: 2538 Dimensions: Width 68' - 8" Depth 64' - 8"

PRIVATE COVERED DECK

Eastridge~

- wide-open formal dining room and great room provide tremendous living space

- bayed dinette blends into huge hearth room with fireplace and built-in cabinets

- atrium door takes you from luxurious master bedroom onto covered deck

- secondary bedrooms complemented by private bath with two vanities

- ORDER NO. EL 2581 - PRICE CODE 25

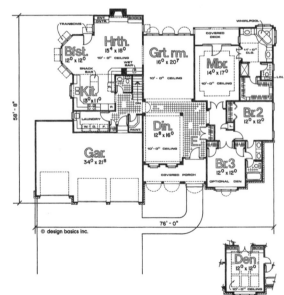

Total Square Footage: 2558 Dimensions: Width 76' - 0" Depth 58' - 8" Optional Den

GRANDEUR WITHIN

Royale~

- fantastic kitchen features pass-thru buffet to dining room, 2 lazy Susans and shares snack bar with spacious breakfast area

- side entrance from covered porch located rear kitchen and laundry facilities

- dazzling rear elevation created by skylit covered porch with arched windows and French doors to master suite and entry hall

- luxurious trend continues in master suite with oval whirlpool bath, exceptional his and her vanities and ample walk-in closet

- ORDER No. EL 3045 - PRICE CODE 25

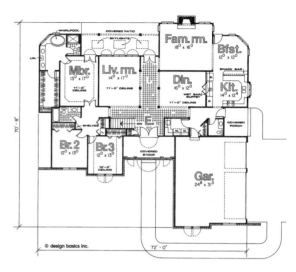

Total Square Footage: 2598 Dimensions: Width 72' - 0" Depth 70' - 8"

RICHLY APPOINTED

Del Ray~

- formal entertaining areas defined by ceiling treatments and flooring materials

- living room, master bedroom and dinette/family room offer outside access to covered patios

- master bath's sunken oval whirlpool under canopy of dramatic sloped ceiling is surrounded by windows

- ORDER No. EL 2834 - PRICE CODE 26

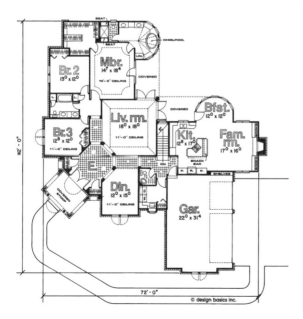

Total Square Footage: 2651 Dimensions: Width 72' - 0" Depth 82' - 0"

FAMILY SHOWCASE

Westmont~

- great room reveals transom windows showcasing a fireplace

- oak breakfast area features bayed windows and 11'-0" ceiling

- kitchen amenities include oak floor three lazy Susans and abundant counter space

- master suite with vaulted 11'-0" ceiling and access to private covered porch

- bedroom #4 converts easily to a den or mother-in-law suite

- ORDER NO. EL 3483 - PRICE CODE 26

Total Square Footage: 2655 Dimensions: Width 66' - 8" Depth 72' - 8"

STUNNING ARCHES

Coronado~

- a series of stunning arches lead from the entry through the volume great room and dining room to the elegant covered veranda

- tall windows flank beautiful fireplace in gathering room with access to covered veranda

- additional outdoor living space provided by private courtyard off master bedroom

- lavish master bedroom includes kitchenette and 2 walk-in closets

- bedrooms #2 and #3 share spacious compartmented bath with 2 lavs

- ORDER NO. EL 2844 - PRICE CODE 27

Total Square Footage: 2716 Dimensions: Width 72' - 0" Depth 64' - 8"

CAPTIVATING COURTYARD

Raleigh~

- integrated design of the kitchen, dinette and family room for family living

- for maximum privacy, double doors seclude the bedroom wing from the rest of the house

- luxury abounds in the richly appointed master suite whose character is enhanced by a private sitting room

• ORDER NO. EL 2580 - PRICE CODE 27

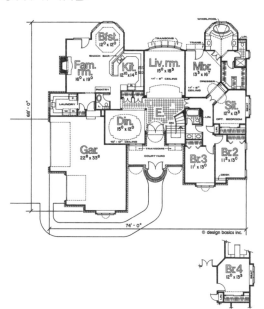

Total Square Footage: 2775 Dimensions: Width 74' - 0" Depth 68' - 0" Optional Bedroom

ELABORATE DETAILS

Avalon~

- 12-foot-tall entry centers on formal living room with fireplace and beautiful arched windows

- large laundry room with double window, freezer space and laundry sink

- informal living enjoyed in spacious family room and breakfast area

- master suite features his and her walk-in closets, a built-in kitchenette and private access to rear yard

• ORDER NO. EL 3033 - PRICE CODE 28

1-800-947-7526
Order Direct

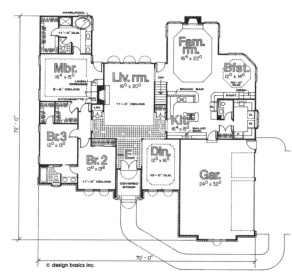

Total Square Footage: 2899 Dimensions: Width 70' - 0" Depth 72' - 0"

ELEGANT ELEVATION

Cornell~

- massive living room with 11'-0" tall ceiling, beautiful arched transoms and French doors with rear access

- secluded den with 11-foot spider beamed ceiling

- kitchen offers a planning desk and angled cabinets with glass doors

- large family room is strategically open to both gazebo breakfast area and kitchen

- master bedroom complemented by bayed sitting area, walk-in closet and access to the back

- Order No. EL 3440 - Price Code 29

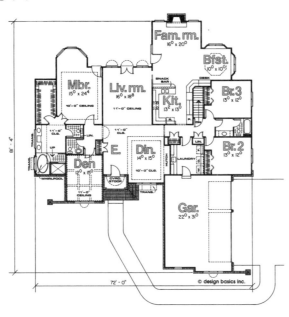

Total Square Footage: 2988 Dimensions: Width 72' - 0" Depth 81' - 4"

PLANTATION-STYLE SPLENDOR

Shiloh~

- gathering room with cathedral ceiling, brick fireplace and entertainment center has useful service porch entrance

- private access to arbor and secluded work space highlight master bedroom

- bedroom #2 can become private study off master bedroom while bedroom #4 easily converts to optional den

- Order No. EL 3018 - Price Code 29

1-800-947-7526
Order Direct

Total Square Footage: 2994 Dimensions: Width 76' - 0" Depth 66' - 8" Optional Den

DO the right thing with our home plans.

If you've ever paid to have a home plan designed from scratch, you know it's expensive – and time consuming. At Design Basics, we invest thousands of dollars and a vast amount of time to painstakingly develop each one of our home plans. But because of our plan service approach, we can offer our award-winning designs for only a fraction of the cost.

WHAT'S the **RIGHT** thing?

Each of our home plans has been registered with the U.S. Copyright Office. Because they're copyrighted, you need to be aware of the following points regarding their proper use.

* If you make modifications to a Design Basics home plan, including the artist's rendering of that home plan, the rights to use of the modified plan and the right to claim of copyright in the modified plan are still governed by Design Basics as owner of the copyright of the original home plan.

   NOTE– regardless of how extensive the changes are, no claim of copyright may be made in any modified Design Basics home plan.

* Redrawing and/or constructing a home that utilizes design elements, either in whole or in part, based on a copyrighted Design Basics home plan, constitutes infringement of U.S. copyright law and can carry penalties of up to $100,000 per violation.

WITH this in mind, please respect our **COPYRIGHTS** !

Gold Seal™ Home Plans

DISPLAY A DREAM

Envision the home of your dreams with our *Color Renderings*. Each of our 11" x 14" renderings are artists' original, hand-colored portrayals of the front elevation and floor plan of the home of your choice. Framed and matted renderings (mounted in a 13" x 16" black metal frame, with a grey marble matte).

Only $99 (#CR). Unframed $79 (#CR).

GET YOUR NAME OUT

Our *Customized Promotional Handout Artwork* is a favorite sales tool among home builders nationwide. Each camera-ready, 8 ½" x 11" master copy comes ready for reproduction, complete with your name, address, telephone number and even company logo, if desired.

Only $69 (#PHA).

SAVE TIME. COMPARE BIDS. TRACK COSTS.

Our *Materials and Estimator's Workbook* is much more than just a materials list. The Workbook is designed to save valuable time in the budgeting process, ensure accurate and comparable bids and help eliminate errors. It also allows you to track projected costs vs. actual expenditures throughout the construction process.

Only $50 (#MEW).

GEAR UP FOR THE CROWDS

Available for any Design Basics plan, each of these useful products are available in our economical *Parade Home Package*. Included in the Parade Home Package is the Materials and Estimator's Workbook, a Full-Color Rendering, Customized Promotional Handout Artwork and an acrylic literature holder, great for displaying your Promotional Handout copies.

Only $149 (#PHP).

TAKE THE GUESSWORK OUT OF FRAME WORK

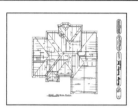
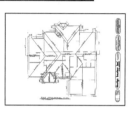

Save time and money with our **Roof Construction Package**. Available for each Design Basics plan, this complete roof framing and dimensional layout includes: 1) Aerial views of the roof showing hips, valleys, ridges, rafters and roof supports. 2) A dimensional plan showing lengths, runs, ridge heights and wall plate heights.

Only $150 (#RCP).

UNDERSTAND OUR PLANS — INSIDE AND OUT

For many home buyers, visualizing the finished home is a challenge. Our **Study Print & Furniture Layout Guide** makes it easy. First, the Study Print provides views of all exterior elevations. Secondly, the Furniture Layout Guide helps them get a "feel" for room sizes, with a ¼" scale floor plan, over 100 reusable furniture pieces and helpful tips on space planning. Available for any Design Basics plan.

Only $29.95 (#SP).

COMPLETE YOUR HOME PLAN LIBRARY

Discover 442 home plan ideas with a set of **Gold Seal™ Home Plan Books** from Design Basics. Included are award-winning one-story, 1 ½ and 2-story homes in popular square footage ranges. Custom changes are available for all.

Gold Seal™ Plan Books — set of 5 for $84.95 (#900R)
or $19.95 each

Homes of Distinction — 86 plans under 1800' (#901R)
Homes of Sophistication — 106 plans, 1800' - 2199' (#902R)
Homes of Elegance — 107 plans, 2200' - 2599' (#903R)
Homes of Prominence — 75 plans, 2600' - 2999' (#904R)
Homes of Grandeur — 68 plans, 3000' - 4000' (#905R)

perfect

(pur′fekt),
adj. 1. complete in all respects; flawless
2. excellent, as in skill or quality.

home plan

(hōm) (plan),
n. 1. technical drawings that impart information
and visual perspectives necessary for the
construction of a home.

design basics custom change

(di zin′)(bā′siks)(kus′ təm)(chānj),
n. 1. modification to a Design Basics plan
as specified by a customer.

Everyone has their own definition of the perfect home plan. At Design Basics, our Custom Change Division can help turn your definition into a reality. Whether you'd like to enlarge a bedroom, modify a garage, or include a finished basement, we can change any of our plans to meet your specifications. Call 800-947-7526 for more information.

design basics inc
HOME PLAN DESIGN SERVIC

Timeless Legacy™

Within Timeless Legacy™ one-story homes, beauty, spaciousness and luxury await those who choose to live in them. Stately elevations of understated elegance distinguish the look of each design. Beautiful windows are given special placement for an abundance of natural light and views to the outside, creating an open, airy feel inside the homes. To further take advantage of outdoor vistas, each of the designs in this collection offers front and rear porches. Comfortable accommodations inside are combined with lavish amenities and intricate detailing throughout all areas of the homes. Arches and angles define many of the rooms to achieve a feeling of openness and easy transition. For added convenience, one of the five designs in this collection has the benefit of a guest suite above the garage to accommodate a live-in nanny or maid. Timeless Legacy™ one-story designs offer exquisite, sprawling floor plans for the luxury homebuyer. Such a unique collection will surely make living in them unforgettable.

THE EDGEWATER

Arches sublime and sequential from exterior to interior. Undefined perimeters from snack bar to fireplace, encouraging ease in daily leisure. A serene rear porch, provoking visits from the breakfast area and master suite.

• ORDER NO. EL 9159 - PRICE CODE 24

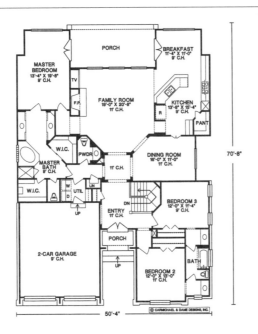

Total Square Footage: 2409 Dimensions: Width 50' - 4" Depth 70' - 8"

THE WHITMORE

A streamlined design that extends in many directions, inherently heightening the number of available outdoor vistas. Communal 12-foot ceilings in the kitchen, breakfast area and family room empower their ease of transition.

• ORDER NO. EL 9120 - PRICE CODE 33

1-800-947-7526
Order Direct

Optional Basement Access

Total Square Footage: 3312 Dimensions: Width 90' - 11" Depth 81' - 3"

WEYBRIDGE MANOR

A rippled coherence of rooms at the rear encourage the essential traffic flow between formal and informal living. An impressionable back porch giving the contemporary comforts of an outdoor servery/bar. And, above the garage, a private guest suite.

- ORDER NO. EL 9128 – PRICE CODE 35

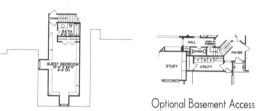

Total Square Footage: 3587 Dimensions: Width 93' - 11" Depth 72' - 3"

Optional Basement Access

VILLA DE BACA

Though distinctly French Colonial, there is an authentic note of independence in its design. A sun-filled loggia exaggerates the living room, which is bound to the kitchen and hearth room by a see-through fireplace set in arches.

- ORDER NO. EL 9118 – PRICE CODE 35

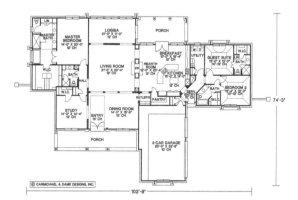

Optional Basement Access

Total Square Footage: 3590 Dimensions: Width 102' - 9" Depth 74' - 3"

THE AUTUMN VIEW

Sleek, marble flooring in the octagonal foyer stretches along the gallery and openly meets the hard, wooden flooring of the columned living and dining rooms. The fundamentally comfortable family area shapes a core at the rear of the home.

• ORDER NO. EL 9139 - PRICE CODE 37

Total Square Footage: 3734 Dimensions: Width 98' - 1" Depth 77' - 11"

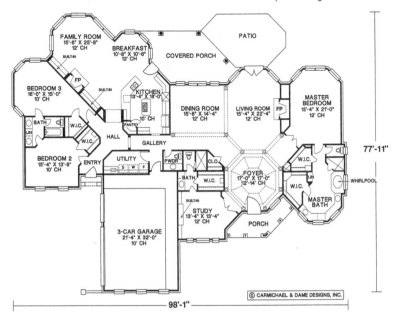

77'-11"

98'-1"

© CARMICHAEL & DAME DESIGNS, INC.

FAMILY ROOM 15'-8" X 25'-8" 12' CH
BREAKFAST 10'-8" X 10'-8" 12' CH
PATIO
COVERED PORCH
BEDROOM 3 16'-0" X 15'-0" 10' CH
KITCHEN 13'-4" X 18'-0"
DINING ROOM 15'-8" X 14'-4" 12' CH
LIVING ROOM 15'-4" X 22'-4" 12' CH
MASTER BEDROOM 15'-4" X 21'-0" 12' CH
BATH
LIN
W.I.C.
W.I.C.
HALL
PANTRY
GALLERY
BEDROOM 2 15'-4" X 13'-8" 10' CH
ENTRY
UTILITY
PWDR
CLO.
FOYER 17'-0" X 17'-0" (12'-14' CH)
W.I.C.
LIN
BATH
W.I.C.
W.I.C.
WHIRLPOOL
STUDY 13'-4" X 13'-4" 12' CH
MASTER BATH
3-CAR GARAGE 21'-4" X 32'-0" 10' CH
PORCH

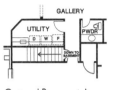

GALLERY
UTILITY
PWDR
DOWN TO BASEMENT

Optional Basement Access

Carmichael & Dame PRODUCT REVIEW

PRESENT YOUR HOME IN WATERCOLOR

Carmichael & Dame present **Timeless Portraits**, distinct watercolor renderings available for each of their superb designs. This 24" x 20" Gallery Presentation is available on an emerald matte with a linen accent enclosed in a gold frame. Each rendering can be adapted to include the name of the builder and/or customer.

Just $150.00 (#CR)

STUDY THE PLAN - BEFORE YOU BUY

Carmichael & Dame's **HOME PLAN STUDY PRINT** is available on any of their 58 stunning designs. Includes large views of all four exterior elevations and floor plans. Although it lacks sufficient detail for construction purposes, this study print provides an excellent opportunity to understand the design inside and out – before buying the plan.

Only $25 (#CDSP).

HANDS OF A CRAFTSMAN — HEART OF A DESIGNER

Timeless Legacy™, A Collection of Fine Home Designs by Carmichael & Dame, includes water color renderings of 52 breathtakingly crafted plans from 3300 to 4500 square feet. Both slab and basement foundations are included with each plan. Each home has been built by Carmichael & Dame's home building division. Available for $25 (#9005R). A leather hardbound, limited edition is also available for $50 (#9015R).

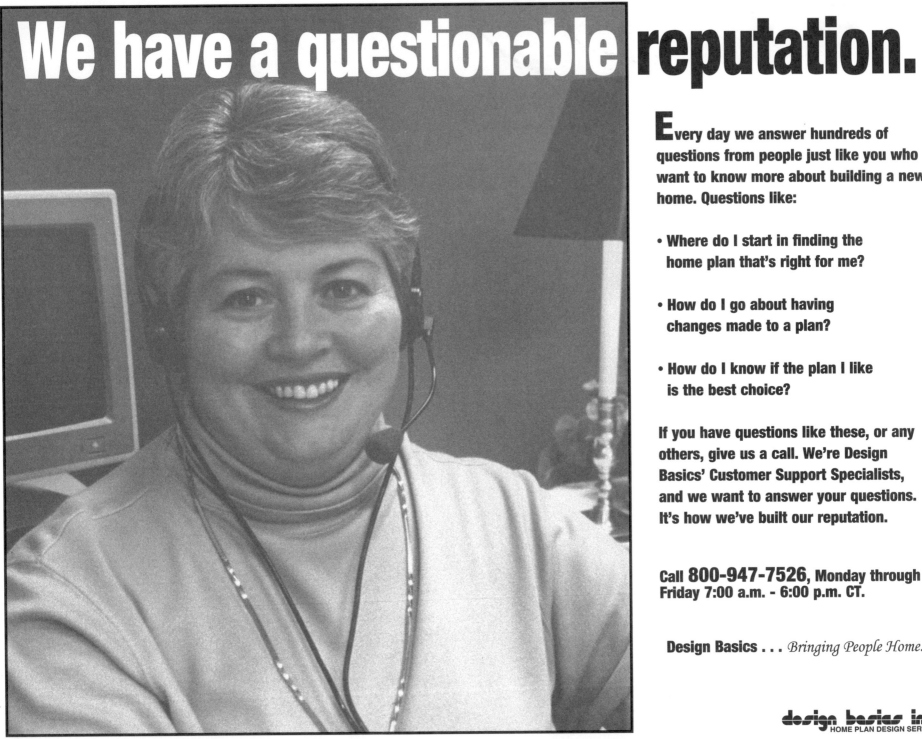

We have a questionable reputation.

Every day we answer hundreds of questions from people just like you who want to know more about building a new home. Questions like:

• Where do I start in finding the home plan that's right for me?

• How do I go about having changes made to a plan?

• How do I know if the plan I like is the best choice?

If you have questions like these, or any others, give us a call. We're Design Basics' Customer Support Specialists, and we want to answer your questions. It's how we've built our reputation.

Call **800-947-7526**, Monday through Friday 7:00 a.m. - 6:00 p.m. CT.

Design Basics . . . *Bringing People Home.*

design basics inc.®
HOME PLAN DESIGN SERVICE

Name	Address
	(Packages cannot be shipped to a P.O. Box.)
Company	Above address is a ☐ business address ☐ residence address
Title	City _____ State _____ Zip _____
☐ Visa [VISA] ☐ AMEX [Card]	Phone ( ) _____ FAX ( ) _____
☐ MasterCard [MasterCard] ☐ Discover [DISCOVER NOVUS]	[⬚⬚⬚⬚⬚⬚⬚⬚⬚⬚⬚⬚⬚⬚ ⬚⬚⬚]
☐ Check enclosed	Expiration Date

(All COD's must be paid by Certified Check, Cashier's Check or Money Order. – Additional $5.00 charge on COD orders)

Signature _____

Order Direct (800) 947-7526

Monday - Friday 7 a.m. to 6 p.m. C.T.

OR **FAX** YOUR ORDER TO US ANYTIME AT **(402) 331-5507**

Follow this example for ordering PLANS:

EL-8018	Forest Glen	$415
PLAN NUMBER	**PLAN NAME**	**TOTAL**
Additional set of prints w/plan purchase	ea. $10.00	
	SUBTOTAL	

Follow this example for ordering PLAN PRODUCTS:

MEW – EL-8018	Study Print & Furniture Layout Guide	1	$29.95
PRODUCT CODE – PLAN NUMBER	**DESCRIPTION**	**QTY.**	**TOTAL**
BOOK CODE	**BOOK NAME**	**QTY.**	**TOTAL**

SHIPPING & HANDLING
(CONTINENTAL US)

Home plans
2nd Business Day . . . . N/C
Next Business Day $15.00

Books & Products
UPS Ground (4-5 business days) . . . . $ 4.95
2nd Business Day $10.00
Next Business Day $20.00
Any Single Plan Book . . . . $ 2.95
Any Combination of Plan Books . . . . $ 4.95

SAME DAY SHIPPING IF ORDERED BY 2:00 P.M. CT.

SUBTOTAL OF PLANS, PRODUCTS AND BOOKS	
NE Res. Add 6.5% Tax	
TX Res. Add 6.25% Tax (plan purchases only)	
◄ Shipping & Handling (see chart at left)	
Total	

No refunds or exchanges, please.
All orders payable in U.S. funds only.

All Design Basics home plans come with a basement foundation. Carmichael & Dame home plans come with both basement and slab foundations. Alternate foundations available for additional charges. Home plans do not carry an architect's/engineer's stamp. You may need to obtain an architect's/engineer's stamp to comply with your local building codes.

HOME PLAN PRICE SCHEDULE

Plan Price Code	1 Set Master Vellums		
	HEARTLAND	**GOLD SEAL**	**CARMICHAEL & DAME**
09		$425	
10		$435	
11		$445	
12	$355	$455	
13	$365	$465	
14	$375	$475	
15	$385	$485	
16	$395	$495	
17	$405	$505	
18	$415	$515	
19	$425	$525	
20	$435	$535	
21	$445	$545	
22	$455	$555	
23	$465	$565	
24	$475	$575	
25		$585	
26		$595	
27		$605	
28		$615	
29		$625	
24			$540
33			$730
34			$740
35			$750
36			$760
37			$770

Construction License

When you purchase a Design Basics or Carmichael & Dame home plan, you'll receive a Construction License which gives you certain rights in building the home depicted in that plan, including:

Running blueprints: Your home plans are sent to you on vellum paper that reproduces well on a blueprint machine. The Construction License authorizes you or your blueprint facility, at your direction, to make as many copies of the plan from the vellum masters as you need for construction purposes.

Local modifications: The Construction License allows you to make modifications to your home plans. We offer a complete custom change service, or you may have the desired changes done locally by a qualified draftsman, designer, architect, or engineer.

No re-use fee: As the original plan buyer, the Construction License permits you to build the plan as many times as you like.

design basics inc.
HOME PLAN DESIGN SERVICE

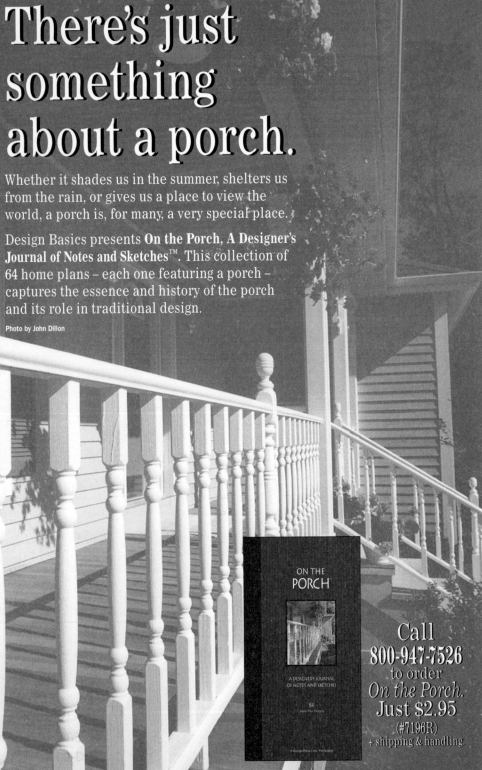